THE COMPLETE
HUNTER™

MULE DEER
Hunting

By **Jim Zumbo**
Hunting Editor for Outdoor Life *Magazine*

CREATIVE
PUBLISHING
international

MINNETONKA, MINNESOTA
www.howtobookstore.com

Jim Zumbo, an outdoor writer since the mid-1960s, has hunted mule deer throughout the western U.S. and Canada. Zumbo currently serves as Hunting Editor for *Outdoor Life* magazine. He lives near Cody, Wyoming, and takes joy in hunting with his wife, son and three daughters.

CREATIVE
PUBLISHING
international

MULE DEER HUNTING
By Jim Zumbo

Executive Editor, Outdoor Products Group: David R. Maas
Managing Editor: Jill Anderson
Senior Editor and Project Leader: Steven J. Hauge
Creative Director: Bradley Springer
Senior Art Director: David W. Schelitzche
Photo Editor and Project Manager: Angela Hartwell
Studio Manager: Marcia Chambers
Studio Photographers: Tate Carlson, Andrea Rugg
Director, Production Services: Kim Gerber
Production Manager: Helga Thielen
Production Staff: Laura Hokkanen, Stephanie Barakos
Cover Photo: Michael H. Francis
Contributing Photographers: Erwin & Peggy Bauer, Kathy S. Butt, Tim Christie, Michael H. Francis, D. Robert Franz, Donald M. Jones, Mark Kayser, Lee Kline, Gary Kramer, Bill McRae, Wyman Meinzer, George Robbins, Wendy Shattil & Bob Rozinski, Dusan Smetana, Ron Spomer
Contributing Manufacturers: Boone and Crockett Club - Jack and Susan Reneau, Chris Tonkinson; Brunton; Burris Sport Optics - Mark Woyak; Irish Setter Sport Boots - Stephanie Elsen, Kim Emery; The Outdoor Connection (The Padded Super Sling) - Brian Tommerdahl; Remington Arms Company, Inc. - Teressa Carter, Linda Powell

Printing: R. R. Donnelley & Sons Co.
10 9 8 7 6 5 4 3 2 1

Copyright © 2001 by Creative Publishing international, Inc.
5900 Green Oak Drive
Minnetonka, MN 55343
1-800-328-3895
www.howtobookstore.com

Library of Congress Cataloging-in-Publication Data

Zumbo, Jim.
    Mule deer hunting / by Jim Zumbo.
        p. cm. -- (The Complete hunter)
    ISBN 0-86573-156-X (hardcover)
    1. Mule deer hunting. I. Title. II. Complete hunter (Creative Publishing International)

  SK301 .Z86 2001
  799.2'7653--dc21

                            2001028967

Contents

Introduction

Mention mule deer to most hunters outside the West and you'll likely get various reactions: big ears, big antlers, dumb, and easy to hunt. The first two observations are true; the latter are false. Muleys have earned the unfortunate reputation of being pushovers, probably because they were in fact exactly that – 3 decades ago. Now, mule deer are far more sophisticated than they were in the old days, simply because they've progressed through an amazing evolutionary transition that has resulted in a new breed, so to speak.

When I first started hunting muleys in the early 1960s, it was nothing to tip over huge bucks that stood boldly and fearlessly in the open. Those deer were naïve, and completely unwary. They stared innocently at hunters, blissfully ignorant of danger.

Now, you'll do well to find a mature buck that's as trusting as he was in those banner years. He'll evaporate like a wispy strand of fog, and will be as elusive as any whitetail you've ever laid eyes on. Modern muleys have earned a PhD in wariness, and that education spanned just a few decades.

Why so, you ask? What's changed so profoundly to steer these animals into a gene pool that reeks with a sudden almost-genius mentality? I think that we need to look at some very basic presumptions: deer that were dumb were easily removed from the pool, and the survivors learned, by necessity, how to stay alive, pure and simple.

Despite that evaluation, mule deer are still considered far less wary than whitetails, their close cousins. To be fair, there's a logical explanation, rooted in behavior patterns as well as the nature of the environment in which they live. Muleys aren't as nervous as whitetails by nature, and seem to be more relaxed and laid back when they feed and travel. And just as importantly, mule deer indeed live in more open country, where their defense is often dependent on their ability to see danger from a distance. In that regard, the muley has learned to live in a habitat where vision is a vital survival factor. Instead of running through heavy cover to escape, as the whitetail does, the mule deer might hesitate to take stock of the disturbance that alerted it. Whatever you think of the mule deer's intelligence, be aware that harvest statistics show that plenty of hunters continue to go home each year without their deer. In some of our top mule deer states, only 30 percent or so of the hunters are successful. Looking at it from another perspective, 70 out of 100 hunters fail to get their deer each year.

Bottom line is the fact that mule deer are a challenging quarry and more hunters are becoming aware of that as they seek this uniquely western deer. In that regard, I've tried to describe in this book the strategies that work best, as well as define each of the many habitats the muley dwells in along with the techniques that are most successful in those environments.

I've also addressed the many facets of mule deer hunting, whether you're a novice or veteran – from planning a hunt, to hiring an outfitter, to gear, guns, bows and ammo, and everything else that will make you a better hunter. Treat the modern mule deer as a worthy and intelligent quarry, as he is, and you'll be much closer to punching your tag. But treat him as a "dumb" animal as we did a few decades ago, and you'll likely go home empty-handed. Many hunters learn that distressing fact of life every year in mule deer country.

Hopefully these pages will help you understand everything you need to know about mule deer and how to be one of the successful hunters who manages to tie a tag to the buck of the West.

Understanding
Mule Deer

Mule Deer Basics

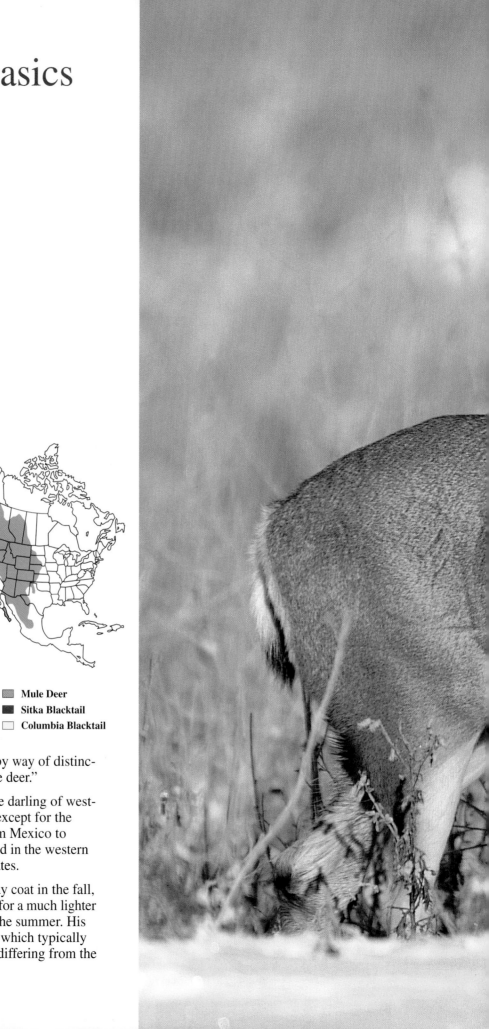

Anyone who has ever seen a mule deer will immediately understand why this western animal was so named. Its ears are disproportionately large, similar to those of a mule. Most wildlife professionals credit Lewis and Clark with giving the deer its name.

Mule Deer
Sitka Blacktail
Columbia Blacktail

William Clark wrote in *The Journal of Lewis and Clark* on March 11, 1806: "The ears and tail of this animal when compared with those of the common (whitetail) deer, so well comported with those of the mule when compared with the horse, that we have by way of distinction adopted the appellation of mule deer."

The muley, also spelled mulie, is the darling of western hunters. He lives nowhere else except for the western part of North America, from Mexico to Canada, in all the western states, and in the western parts of many of the midwestern states.

The mule deer typically wears a gray coat in the fall, winter and early spring, but sheds it for a much lighter pelt, almost a dull orange color, in the summer. His trademarks are his outsized antlers, which typically have a double fork on each antler, (differing from the

Rocky Mountain mule deer

Desert mule deer

whitetail, which has tines coming off main beams), as well as the huge 10-inch (or longer) ears and light-colored rump. His tail is thick, rope-like and is white with a black tip. (below)

The scientific name of the mule deer is *Odocoileus hemionus*, and is attributed to Constantine Samuel Rafinesque, a French-American naturalist. In 1832, Rafinesque first named the whitetail he studied in Virginia as *Odontocoelus*, which is the Greek definition of the deer's concave tooth. Later, the word, which is the genus name, was changed to *Odocoileus*, and when he classified the mule deer afterward, he assigned the species name as *hemionus*, which means mule.

There are several mule deer subspecies in North America; the number may vary depending on the wildlife expert you talk to. Anywhere from seven to eleven subspecies are bandied about, including two subspecies of blacktail deer, which are closely related to mule deer. It's impossible to define exact boundaries of the subspecies because of the widescale disagreements. Suffice to say the blacktail dwells along

the West Coast from California to Alaska, with two very definite subspecies, the Columbian blacktail in the south and the Sitka blacktail in the north. The rest are one form or another of mule deer that live everywhere from Mexico to Canada. The Rocky Mountain mule deer, *Odocoileus hemionus hemionus*, is by far in the majority, with a range at least three times the size of the range of all the rest put together. All of the other subspecies live in the southwest with the most popular being the desert mule deer, *Odocoileus hemionus crooki*.

Mule deer are often thought to be far bigger than whitetails, but that's not the case. Northern deer of either species are very large, often exceeding 250 pounds on the hoof. And as with whitetails, the smallest mule deer live in the South.

The mule deer is exceedingly adaptable, living in environments from sea level to alpine habitat above timberline. It can withstand temperature extremes at both the high and low ends; however, it is extremely vulnerable to prolonged winters with deep snow and severe cold spells. Mule deer will migrate to lower elevations in mountain country, spending upwards of half a year on winter ranges. Their survival during severe winters is generally based on the available forage on those critical wintering areas. Many winter range areas make up less than 10 percent of the deer's entire home range, predisposing them to predation, disease and parasites because they're so concentrated.

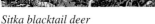
Sitka blacktail deer

Columbia blacktail deer

Mule deer breed in late fall, typically from mid-November to mid-December. After a gestation period of about 6 months, does give birth to fawns in May and June. Twin fawns are not uncommon.

Unlike whitetails, mule deer do not make scrapes, and rubs on trees aren't as prevalent. Mule deer bucks may remain with a herd of does for several days, unlike whitetail bucks, which cover more ground seeking scattered does here and there.

Mule deer, like all members of the deer family, have a four-part stomach, and typically feed late in the afternoon, most of the evening and early in the morning. During the day they bed in and around brush, timber or other vegetative cover, and chew their cuds.

Mule deer have a peculiar gait when fleeing from danger. Called *stotting*, it's a pogo-stick type of bounding. Stotting is thought to allow deer to spot crouching predators more easily as they jump high off the ground.

Several predators pursue mule deer. The mountain lion is probably the most

Mule deer doe and fawn

significant almost everywhere the deer lives. Lions are extremely efficient predators and may kill up to one deer per week, though some biologists believe that number is too high. Whatever the case, lions may have a serious impact on herds during years when deer numbers are low and the habitat is impaired by severe weather. Coyotes kill mule deer, particularly fawns, but have been known to take adults, especially when deer are weakened by the ravages of winter. Black bears, grizzlies and wolves also prey on mule deer, and in some cases bobcats are known to take fawns.

Unlike most other big-game populations in North America, mule deer populations are lower now than they were 20 years ago. Habitat loss is the chief factor; this subject is detailed more fully in the population chapter (p. 30).

Mule deer vocalize far less than whitetails. Fawns may bleat when in distress or separated from their mothers. Does also issue a bleat or a blatt, and bucks grunt, especially during the rut. Both bucks and does snort when alarmed.

13

Age, Growth & Antler Development

AGE

Mule deer bucks seldom reach much more than 3 years of age in areas of heavy hunting pressure, particularly near good access on public land, and on private land where hunter numbers are high. If deer can maintain vigor by foraging on high-quality food, they may live more than 10 years, but those are very rare individuals. In most of their range muleys must cope with severe winters, a variety of predators, and diseases. Survival is difficult, regardless of the forage. Does live longer than bucks only because they aren't specifically selected as bucks are. Does that are 6 to 10 years old are not uncommon in many herds.

A deer's age is determined only by carefully inspecting its teeth. The amount of wear is a gauge, but is not always reliable. Deer that live in sandy areas, for example, may have abnormal and excessive wear on their teeth because of the grinding action of the sand. On the other hand, deer that eat soft foods much of the time may not have much tooth wear. The only reliable technique is to cross-section a tooth and examine it in a laboratory. In any case, it takes a trained biologist to determine a deer's age, whether it's done in the field or under a microscope.

There is absolutely no way to tell a deer's age by its antlers. A spike or a forked-horn might be a yearling, but then again, it might not, depending on the vigor and condition of the animal.

GROWTH

Mule deer growth depends on several factors, including age, availability and quality of forage, subspecies and the latitude in which they live. It stands to reason that older deer are bigger deer because they're more mature, but that's not necessarily true. A buck in the prime of his life, which is 5 to 7 years old, may be heavier than a buck living in the same area that's 10 years old or more. As animals get old, they lose vigor and lose weight. Dominant rutting bucks will lose weight from the breeding activity, and may continue to be on the light side throughout the winter if the weather is severe. Most weight gain will occur the following spring and early summer.

A deer's subspecies is important in its growth and ultimate weight. Blacktails, for example, are smaller than the Rocky Mountain mule deer that may live fairly close.

Latitude is an important factor in the size of any mammal, not only deer. According to Bergman's Rule, a biological principle, animals that live in northern latitudes are larger than those living in more southerly latitudes. By way of explanation, Bergman's Rule states that animals living in the North are subjected to colder temperatures and are thus bigger in body mass in order to survive. The larger the animal, the less heat loss per square inch of body surface. This rule is easily proven by merely observing mule deer from north to south. Canadian muleys are by far much bigger than Texas muleys, for example – in fact, you can make the same comparison with any mammals that live in widely varying latitudes.

An adult mule deer buck in Canada may weigh 300 pounds or more on the hoof. The very first muley I shot in northern Utah in 1963 weighed 232 dressed on accurate scales. I've taken 70 or 80 more muleys since, and none have been any bigger. According to research done in Wyoming, yearling buck muleys averaged 129 pounds, 2-year-old deer weighed an average of 170 pounds, bucks that were 3 to 5 averaged 206 pounds, and bucks that were 6 years or more averaged 249 pounds. In every age class, does were significantly lighter. These ages are representative of mule deer elsewhere in the northern Rockies.

Statistics are scant for the birth weights of fawns in the wild, but a study of pen-raised animals revealed that the average birth weight of 79 male fawns was 8.3 pounds, and the average birth weight of 93 female fawns was 8 pounds. When they were 135 days old, the male fawns weighed 69 to 80 pounds.

ANTLER DEVELOPMENT

Buck fawns have no distinct antlers, but a close look will reveal small nubbins when deer are 6 months out. These deer are often called button bucks, and will grow "real" antlers during the next spring and summer. Those first appendages may be spikes, fork-horns, or, in some cases, six-point or better racks. The typical mature mule deer has a tall rack, each antler having two double forks and an eyeguard or brow tine. The latter is usually very short, compared to that of whitetails, or may be missing entirely.

Western deer are described according to the points on each antler. For example, a buck with double forks is called a "four-point," and the brow tine is ignored. A buck with four points on one side and three on the other is called a "four by three." In comparison, eastern hunters describe whitetails according to the total number of points. Be wary of regulations if you're hunting a unit that has a minimum antler restriction, since every state has its individual interpretation of what constitutes points. I recall a hunt in Wyoming that had a four-point antler restriction in the unit I hunted. I was a nonresident at the time, and wasn't familiar with details, which was no excuse. On opening morning I turned down three huge muleys, all of them three-pointers. For the life of me, I couldn't find a fourth point on any of those bucks. Later, I related the story to a game warden who seemed surprised, and asked if any of the bucks had brow tines. They indeed did, and the warden told me that in Wyoming the brow tine is a legal point. That wasn't the case in Utah, where I lived at the time, so I was blissfully ignorant of the law.

In the early spring, usually in April, antlers start to appear and grow rapidly. As they grow, they're covered by a sheath that we call "velvet," which protects the very fragile rack. By August, the antlers are fully grown, and increasing testosterone levels in the buck induce the velvet to peel away. Contrary to popular belief, the buck does not need to vigorously rub his antlers to eliminate the velvet. For the most part, this material is shed easily, leaving behind a rack that may be reddish or streaked with red. The buck immediately rubs his antlers on vegetation, changing the color of the antler to a brownish-tan color, the shade depending on the type of vegetation the buck is rubbing. By late August and early September, the velvet is completely gone. Bucks that live in open habitats often have very light-colored antlers, caused by bleaching from the sun. Conversely, bucks that dwell in the timber and brush usually have dark-colored antlers. As testosterone levels drop, usually in January, the antlers are shed, and usually the most vigorous bucks shed their antlers first. On winter ranges, discarded antlers are easily found by shed collectors, and often a pair will be found lying close to each other. Hunting for antlers is a sport in itself, and has many followers these days. Some antlers are used for furniture, or are sold for the aphrodisiac trade, or are simply displayed in homes as art forms.

Non-typical antlers are a fairly common occurrence throughout the range of the mule deer. Although injuries to the antlers during their development will cause irregularities, it has also been shown that other injuries can also cause antlers to grow in non-typical fashion. The most common cause of this type of antler growth is through genetics. Non-typical mule deer antlers can show up anywhere, but because this trait can be passed down through generations there are often areas that are known for producing larger numbers of these unique trophies (opposite page).

MULE DEER BUCKS shed their velvet in the late summer.

Non-Typical Antlers

Mule deer commonly wear antlers that don't conform to the standard configuration. These antlers may have extra points, they may have so-called "drop tines," and they may come in bizarre shapes and forms. There are enough of these offbeat antlers that the Boone and Crockett Club has a special designation for them in the record book.

A number of factors cause antlers to be "different." One is simply based on genetics. Ancestry is an important element in antler design; in some areas, a disproportionate number of bucks may have non-typical racks because of heredity. In some parts of Arizona and Utah, for example, many mature bucks are non-typicals. Some hunters are especially attracted to freak racks and seek them out in areas where they're historically found.

Non-typical racks may also be caused by an injury. A wound to the left side of the buck will cause the right antler to be deformed; conversely, an injury to the right side will result in the left antler being deformed.

It's been documented that a deer's diet will cause deformed antlers. This occurs in regions where necessary trace elements are either inadequate or totally lacking.

The testosterone levels in a buck's body are important in antler growth. There are cases where an injury to a buck's testicles will cause profound effects on his overall growth as well as the configuration of his antlers. This is the reason that domestic animals have their testicles removed. Steers, for example, are bulls minus their testicles.

In the early 1960s, I took a very large-bodied muley buck in Utah that had a bizarre rack with antlers entirely encased in velvet. I shot the deer in late October, when the velvet should have been gone for 2 months or so. When I field-dressed the buck, I was astounded to see that his testicles were absent. Ironically, a hunting buddy killed a similar buck a couple days later. It too had a freak rack covered with velvet, and its testicles were also gone.

Rumor had it that cowboys on the range occasionally roped fawn deer, and if they were bucks, the animals were castrated. It should be remembered that this was a time when mule deer were at the peak of their populations and considered vermin by many ranchers. It also should be realized that cowboys often have a strange sense of humor. Whatever the case, I'm convinced those bucks had freak racks because they had no testicles, which is borne out by the observations of others who are familiar with mule deer.

Some antlers resemble cactus or a piece of coral, with no real distinctive shape. These are probably caused by hereditary factors. Drop tines are favored by many hunters, and bucks carrying them are also affected by genes.

Non-typical antlers usually don't show up until a buck is about three years old (if from ancestral causes), or the year after a wound occurs. In most cases, a buck with freak antlers will retain that general shape year after year. The rack is shed, and a new pair of non-typical antlers will grow immediately afterward.

Muleys with unique antlers will be around as long as there are mule deer. Very few hunters are disappointed when they take one, and, in many cases, those heads will be proudly displayed on a wall.

Mule Deer Habitat

Trying to define the muley's habitat would be virtually impossible, for the deer of the West is quite at home practically everywhere. You'll find them in lowland, arid deserts, to arctic environments above timberline. Between those two extremes, mule deer will be quite at home in farmlands, along river corridors, in aspen and evergreen forests, and in brush and scrub oak thickets.

Because the western deer are chiefly browsers, you're apt to see them in places where there's plenty of brush, which is their chief forage. But plenty of deer live in the so-called "black timber," dense forests composed of pines, spruces, firs and other evergreens.

The blacktail deer of the West Coast dwell in the densest, nastiest, most impenetrable country on the continent. This is a land of heavy rainfall, and forests that literally cannot be penetrated without a machete or axe. In this extreme country, many hunters opt to hunt blacktails in clearcuts where visibility is better and travel is easier, though second-growth clearcuts can be thick jungles. The easy way to hunt blacktails is to watch for them from log landings, which are clearings usually located on the edge of a slope where you can see a fair distance below. Hunters who elect to hunt this West Coast animal have their work literally cut out for them, and in my opinion are the toughest deer hunters in the country. Competition is extremely heavy around log landings in public forests, but much less where the roads are closed by locked gates, requiring a long walk in.

Muleys that live in deserts or open forests with scattered trees are far easier to locate than deer in other

habitats. Quaking aspen forests standing naked with their leaves gone in late fall are also good places to spot muleys without a great degree of difficulty. Farms and ranches attract muleys like magnets, and their crops are feasted upon by hungry deer. Here, deer readily expose themselves in fields, but hunting may not be allowed in those areas.

Habitats are largely governed by two basic factors, their latitude and elevation. In the higher elevations, for example, rimrock and dwarf trees offer a very cold, often open environment. As you progress down the mountain, you'll find evergreens, then aspens, then high brush, then pinyons and junipers, and finally sagebrush and high desert.

You won't find many aspen, scrub oak, or pinyons and cedars in the northern states, and open parks and clearings might not be as numerous as in the central and more southerly Rocky Mountain states. In Oregon and Washington, the difference between the east and west regions is like night and day. The west is characterized by heavy, wet forests; the east is far more arid. The Cascade Range in the middle is the transition between the two. California habitats also vary enormously, depending on the region.

Mule deer are commonly linked to sagebrush, regardless of the habitat they live in. If you find sagebrush, you'll undoubtedly locate muleys. I recall a combo elk/deer hunt with a pal who was more interested in mule deer. He was an extremely knowledgeable hunter, and focused all his attention on a knob that held the only sagebrush for miles. He took a nice buck from that spot, and neither he nor the rest of us saw a deer anywhere else.

While muleys are considered to be deer of the West, some big bucks are taken from Kansas, Nebraska, and other prairie states. Texas has muleys in the western desert country, and mule deer thrive on farms in both of the Dakotas.

Land ownership in the 11 western states is a mixture of private, state, and federal. In some states, like Nevada, the majority of land is administered by the federal government, notably the Bureau of Land Management. As explained in the chapter on planning a hunt, much of the land in fertile valleys and along river and stream corridors is privately owned. Those spots were prime locations for homesteading when the West was settled.

Because mule deer often live in very dry country, water is a necessary commodity during dry periods. Deer may drink from stock watering ponds, seeps, springs and other sources that aren't obvious. It's not uncommon for muleys to walk several miles to water, especially during the night.

Hunters can determine hidden water sources by talking to government employees who work with the land, such as foresters, range technicians and wildlife biologists. Other excellent sources are ranchers and sheepherders. These folks are intimate with the land their stock lives on, and are invaluable sources of information.

In much of the West, mule deer are highly dependent on critical winter ranges that offer them food during the toughest part of the year. These wintering areas are typically in the lower elevations, where there is far less snow than in higher regions. Sagebrush environments, ranchlands and farms are common places that deer utilize during the winter. I live in an area in northwest Wyoming where muleys are nowhere to be found in the late spring, summer and early fall. Then, like magic, they suddenly appear in early November by the hundreds, and remain in the valley until the following spring when they head back up to the high country to spend the summer.

Unfortunately, an enormous part of this winter habitat has been permanently destroyed in the name of progress. Suburbs, malls and other developments

Blacktail deer habitat

Desert mule deer habitat

now stand where winter range once existed, and the deer are gone for good. Nowhere will mankind attempt to reverse progress, i.e., to tear down buildings and revert land to winter habitat. That thought is ludicrous, and therein lies an enormous problem for mule deer.

Much of the wild lands away from urban centers has likewise been negatively altered by activities such as mining and oil and gas exploration and development. On a happy note, however, those companies are now required to return those lands to habitats similar to or better than those before development. However, most of the roads constructed to reach those areas will remain open, allowing more travel to mule deer country.

Optimum muley habitat will have a mix of security cover, food and water, and those ingredients must be present as the situation demands. Foods should have the correct mix of plants to offer adequate nutrition, and water and cover must be present when the weather is at its worst. Droughts may have a severe impact on deer, as do severe winters.

Deer will congregate in habitats that offer the best food sources. In places burned by fires or logged, muleys will find succulent forbs and browse plants that are encouraged by mineral soil and unprecedented sunlight. Sometimes mule deer country "looks" barren and worthless, but surprising numbers of animals may dwell in those bleak-looking places. I've seen deer in beat-up overgrazed ranges, in deserts where it seemed no deer could possibly survive, and in the high tundra above timberline. Experts try to probe this country, to learn exactly why deer are attracted and indeed survive in it, but no one has all the answers. But it's well-known that the future of mule deer hinges on many factors, good habitat being the key issue. Without proper habitat, mule deer cannot thrive – it's that simple. They may eke out an existence in submarginal country, but there's no substitute for a balance of vital ingredients on excellent habitat.

Because of the completely different habitat types that exist in mule deer country, I break them down into eight major types: desert, sagebrush, agricultural, high brush, riverbottoms, pinyon-juniper, aspen, and evergreen forests. Later in this book I'll describe the vegetative components for each, as well as the most reliable hunting strategies for each.

Be aware that you may see a mule deer practically anywhere in the West. These animals are as tough as any other big-game species out there.

SAGEBRUSH is commonly found in the best mule deer habitats.

Food, Feeding & Digestion

Mule deer are commonly defined as browsers. They have a decided preference for browse, which is defined as shrubs and vegetation that are not grass or forbs. The latter two can make up an important part of their diet during certain times of the year. In some habitats, however, browse may not be an important part of their food intake. A variety of factors make up the dietary requirements, including availability and quantity of forage, and the time of year.

In the spring, deer hungrily consume a wide variety of emerging buds and grasses, after a long winter of mostly eating shrubs that have a comparatively low nutritional value. Newly greening grasses are eagerly sought out, as are forbs and other lush foods. Summer diets include less grass, but more dependence on shrubs and forbs. In many areas, the latter may make up two-thirds of the summer diet. In the autumn, the presence of frost alters the diet, killing many of the forbs and grasses, though fall rains may promote late grass growth and attract deer to this quickly growing food source. Forbs are still high on the menu, but deer begin making a transition to shrubs. In the winter, shrubs make up a large part of the deer's food, amounting to 75 percent or more of the total forage base.

Shrubs that are commonly consumed by mule deer include sagebrush, bitterbrush, rabbitbrush, mountain mahogany, willow, buffaloberry, huckleberries and cinquefoil. These are traditional mainstays, but many more vegetative species are eaten, depending on the habitat.

If any one vegetative species can be keyed on to give a clue to the presence of mule deer, it's sagebrush – hands down. If you're hunting in an evergreen environment, for example, and come across a rare expanse of sagebrush, odds are good that that's where you'll see mule deer. The deer of the West go hand in hand with the most popular and widespread shrub of the West. In many cases, the health and well being of a mule deer herd is dependent of the availability of sagebrush during the winter months. It isn't the mere presence of sagebrush plants that's necessarily important, but the amount of new growth produced in the summer. It's the new growth that offers the most nutritional value that is desperately required by deer during hard times in the winter. In areas where there are ranches

and farms, mule deer may spend a substantial amount of time in the fields, eating yellowed and dried crops such as alfalfa, corn, and other plants. In some cases, deer cause extensive damage to croplands, and wildlife officers typically establish antlerless seasons to keep herds trimmed.

On many western ranges administered by federal agencies, vegetation is managed for livestock, which often compete with mule deer. Domestic sheep are the most competitive of the livestock species. This was a major problem years ago, but agencies are now mandated to provide for wildlife as well. Prescribed burns are often used to enhance mule deer range, and *chaining* projects in pinyon juniper forests eliminated deca-

dent trees and replaced them with quality browse. Chaining involves dragging a huge ship-anchor chain between two bulldozers, thereby tearing up the low-value trees, and then planting seeds that ultimately feed big game, other wildlife and livestock.

Most feeding occurs in late afternoon, throughout the night and early in the morning. Deer may nibble on and off during the day. In places where hunting pressure is heavy, deer are more nocturnal, feeding mostly at night. During severe winter weather, periods of deep snow and extended below-zero temperatures, deer may feed much of the day since it takes longer to obtain forage in deep snow, and plenty of food is needed to get the extra calories required. During

exceptionally severe winters, enormous numbers of mule deer may starve, despite efforts to feed them with items such as hay. The microbes in their stomach aren't capable of digesting unfamiliar forage, and deer literally die with full stomachs.

All members of the deer family ruminate, which means they chew their cuds. Food enters a four-part stomach, the first called the rumen. The initial food is in rough form, and is then regurgitated and chewed. Once it's broken down, it is then processed and digested in the other three stomachs, called the reticulum, the omasum, and the abomasum.

Senses

As you might imagine, the very large ears on the mule deer enable it to hear at long distances. Deer are keenly aware of foreign sounds in their environment, and will immediately look at the source of the sound with their ears at full alert. Mule deer are seemingly more complacent than their more nervous whitetail relatives, but nonetheless have a tremendous ability to hear even the slightest sounds. Though there are no studies that show exactly how good a mule deer's ears are, any hunter who has pursued this western animal is very well aware of this highly tuned sense.

The vision of the mule deer is outstanding; many people feel it's as good as that of a pronghorn antelope. No doubt this sense has evolved so well because these open-country animals must use their eyes to see danger at a distance. Muleys seem to have no problem spotting danger at a half-mile or more. Add to this the habit of deer clustering in herds, and you have a situation where many eyes are available to spot a hunter or animal predator.

The sense of smell also appears to be very well adapted to mule deer's escape as well as breeding requirements. Deer can detect approaching danger by smelling it from a very long distance. In my own observations, I've been betrayed by errant winds a quarter-mile away from the quarry. Muleys also use their sense of smell in a lip-curl fashion (opposite page) to detect the presence of does in estrus. This is called the *flehmen behavior*, and is seen only during the rut.

Mule deer have many enemies, including mountain lions, which stalk close by making a very stealthy advance and then launching a short surprise attack, and coyotes and wolves, which spot deer from a distance and attack by overtaking the quarry. Other predators such as bears and bobcats also will catch and kill mule deer if the opportunity arises. Because of these enemies, mule deer have evolved with three very highly tuned senses to alert them to danger. Many hunters have learned the hard way that the objective of getting within shooting range of the quarry may be a major undertaking.

WOLVES can be a major predator of mule deer.

Breeding Behavior

Mule deer bucks are extremely social, getting along together nicely most of the year. In the summer, they often hang out in bachelor herds, with typically less than half a dozen in a group, but sometimes many more than that. Once I saw more than 20 bucks – all of them mature animals, and a couple in the 30-inch class – when I was bowhunting in Utah. It was late August, and all the bucks still had their velvet wholly intact.

As the summer progresses, bucks undergo a major transformation. Their testosterone level increases, and the velvet coating on their antlers starts sluffing away. Bucks help eliminate it by rubbing on shrubs and saplings, coloring the antlers to a brown or tan hue, depending on the type of vegetation being rubbed. By mid-October in most mule deer country, bucks begin preparing for the breeding season, which usually starts in earnest in early November and peaks around the end of the month. This timetable may vary according to latitude, elevation and subspecies of deer, but is the norm for most mule deer country. Mature bucks begin to disassociate themselves from each other, and travel alone, seeking does in estrus. At this time, their necks noticeably enlarge due to the swelling of their glands. A distinctive and almost overpowering odor is easily discerned when a hunter approaches a rutting buck that he's downed.

Mature bucks go on the prowl during the rut, seeking does in estrus. At times a buck may hang out with a group of does, probably waiting for a female to come into heat, but there's no definite harem-tending as there is with elk. Fighting doesn't seem to be as common among mule deer bucks as it is with whitetails, but nonetheless occurs. Some of these battles can be vicious, sometimes resulting in the death of one of the combatants. A dominant buck doesn't necessarily have to be the animal with the most impressive rack. I learned that lesson while observing a herd of muleys including a half-dozen bucks and a couple dozen does. A very large four-point buck with antlers that easily measured 30 inches was the undisputed leader of the group. He swaggered about, and when he approached a lesser buck, the subdominant deer immediately beat a hasty retreat.

Presently the big buck looked up a nearby slope and was immediately alarmed. Running straight at him was a small buck with three points to the side and a rack that was no more than 16 inches wide. This small buck slammed into the big buck, goring him in the hindquarter, and instead of fighting, the big buck bounded away as fast as he could. For the next two days he slinked around, keeping to himself, and never venturing toward the does who were now being tended by the little buck. Obviously the small buck was extremely aggressive and was dominant in every sense of the word. His comparatively tiny antlers were not handicaps; it was his attitude that made him the champ.

Breeding season often occurs when deer are just arriving at winter ranges from the high country. This being the case, muleys may be concentrated in big herds, especially where they've taken over croplands. With so many does and bucks around, it's inevitable that there will be many sparring matches between bucks. The most aggressive bucks will easily intimidate lesser bucks, and will remain near a doe that's about to come into heat. A buck will likely curl his lip with his head in an uplifted position to literally test the air for the scent of a doe in estrus. Many studies have documented that almost 100 percent of all does in heat are bred by the time the rut is over. In a Canadian study, a mule deer buck was observed breeding seventeen does. Biologists believe that a ratio of one breeding buck per 13 does is adequate to guarantee that all does will be bred.

Bucks will vigorously rub saplings and brush with their antlers during the rut, creating a great deal of noise. Dr. Valerius Geist, a Canadian university professor and acknowledged expert on mule deer, believes bucks create these sounds to offer an auditory challenge to other bucks. By doing so, a noisy buck intimidates an adversary, and may actually drive the opponent off in this bluffing challenge.

After being bred, the doe remains with the herd, and if it's a migrating group, will likely have her fawn on summer range in the high country. Does will typically remain in a group year-round. Once the rut is over, bucks once again become tolerant of each other and remain together. They continue to do so until the following fall when the breeding season approaches once again.

Movement Patterns

In mountain country where deep snows blanket the land, mule deer have no choice but to move to lower elevations where food is available. These migrations are essential for survival, and in some cases deer may move upwards of a hundred miles from summer to winter range. Though deer follow historic routes to reach their ultimate feeding grounds in the low country, they might not make the complete journey if the winter is mild, remaining instead at intermediate elevations. This could be disastrous if a severe spring storm strikes, leaving deer vulnerable in these areas that offer far less protection than traditional winter grounds. Mule deer that live in the southern latitudes may not migrate at all, since snow isn't an important factor in the winter.

As the snow recedes in the spring, deer move up, following the greening slopes. They'll continue until they reach their normal summering areas, which may be close to timberline in the higher reaches of the Rockies. Fawns are often born in the summer range, and deer will remain there until it's time to move back down the following fall.

Deer may also move when pressured by predators, though these are often temporary situations. Mountain lions, wolves and coyotes may disperse animals to peripheral areas. Deer may also be routed by domestic dogs, especially in urban areas or places where winter ranges are being developed and people are moving in.

Daily movements depend on water, forage and hunting pressure. Reaching water can be as easy as a 5-minute walk in country that has plenty of streams and drainages, as in the case of deer that actually live in riparian habitat along rivers and creeks. Water might also be a 5- or 6-mile daily walk away in arid country to reach one of the scarce waterholes in the region. Deer that must expose themselves in open country almost always drink at night, whereas muleys in brush and forest cover may drink late in the afternoon or early in the morning. The availability of forage also dictates a deer's daily movements. If animals are bedded in heavy timber or in a deep canyon where there's little food, the deer may walk for miles to reach forage. In places they may begin their daily journey very late in the afternoon and be back in their bedding area early in the morning. The presence of hunters will move deer, pushing them into security areas where they're least disturbed. Deer may run erratically when they're routed by people, or they might move stealthily into sanctuaries and remain there until hunting activity lessens. Until it does, most deer movement will occur during the hours of darkness.

Mule deer use extensive trail systems, and have primary and secondary trails. Trails may be relatively unimportant, such as those used when traveling from a general widespread feeding area to a bedding area, or they might be very well-defined, such as trails leading to water. In areas where livestock graze, deer commonly follow cattle and sheep trails in their travels. Deer will often have one main trail in the bottom of a canyon or on top of a ridge, but will use secondary trails when they branch out to feed. When migrating, deer may use a single trail for dozens of miles to reach their destination.

Mule Deer Populations

Ernest Thompson Seton, a famous American naturalist, said that there were 10 million mule deer roaming the U.S. when the country was settled. Many biologists believe that number is far too high. How could Seton make those estimates back in those days long before wildlife management came on the scene? There were no census or inventory techniques, and no airplanes, helicopters or vehicles to conduct any credible counts.

It's interesting to note that some early explorers of the West, including the 1804 – 1806 Lewis and Clark expedition, made little mention of mule deer. Many mountain men and trappers frequently spoke of bison, elk, sheep and bears, but made very little reference to mule deer. In some journals, mule deer were conspicuously absent in the diaries that told of wildlife observations and gathering large animals for food. Deer numbers obviously varied according to the locale.

During modern times, mule deer populations began building in the 40s and 50s, peaking in the 60s. There are varied explanations, including intense predator control where coyotes and mountain lions were bountied and maintained at lower populations, a wealth of quality winter ranges, fewer hunters, and in general, better habitat in most mule deer country. For whatever the reasons, hunters, including me, enjoyed the banner years of mule deer in the mid-60s. Deer numbers were at all-time highs in modern history, and big bucks were abundant and not terribly wise.

Then the bottom dropped out. After a disastrous winter in the early 70s, mule deer populations

plummeted and have never returned to their previous levels. From then until now, cycles have apparently occurred, with rises and dips in mule deer numbers. Most of these changes are believed to have been caused by severe winters, excessive predation, diseases, parasites, loss of habitat and other factors. Many wildlife scientists think that mule deer populations have seen their heyday, and that those high numbers of the 50s and 60s will never be seen again.

Mule deer, including their close cousins, the blacktail deer, live from the beaches of the Pacific coast to the farmlands of the Midwest, and from Canada to Mexico. The bulk of them live in the Rocky Mountain states, primarily Idaho, Montana, Wyoming, Utah and Colorado. Every other western state supports plenty of muleys, each of them having widely varying habitats.

The number of mule deer subspecies has been debated by scientists for many years. The most accepted and updated information indicates that there are seven subspecies. The Rocky Mountain mule deer has by far the largest range and lives in the bulk of the West, while the two blacktail subspecies (Sitka and Columbia) inhabit the West Coast from California to Alaska. The other four live in the Southwest, chiefly in California and Mexico.

In summary, despite the warnings by alarmists who believe mule deer are in serious trouble, most scientists agree that while these deer will never reach their peak populations of the 1950s and 1960s, they are here to stay, though their populations will react according to many factors – some of which we can control, and some of which we can't.

Mule Deer Hunting
Equipment

Rifles & Ammunition

Any discussion of mule deer rifles will likely result in a variety of different opinions, simply because it's a time-honored tradition for hunters to argue about the merits of their personal favorite firearms.

I receive plenty of mail from folks who are planning their first mule deer hunt, and are in a quandary as to what to bring. Some of those hunters live in shotgun-only states or counties, and have no clue as to hunting deer with rifles. Others perceive muleys as being bigger and thus harder to bring down than whitetails, and believe they need to "upgrade" their whitetail rifle to a bigger caliber or magnum.

Let me lay to rest some of these concerns. It's true that the average mule deer is undoubtedly larger than a whitetail in Florida, Alabama, or other southern states where whitetails typically run small, but there are plenty of exceptions. I've seen some very large whitetails in the South. But by and large, whitetails and muleys are pretty much the same size. A big whitetail may dress out at 150 to 200 pounds; same with a mule deer. In fact, I've seen plenty of whitetails, notably from midwestern or northern states, that were much bigger than so-called average muleys.

The big difference between the two species is the country in which they live. Because of the openness of much mule deer country, you can expect long shots, far

longer than you'd expect in the eastern or southern woods. But not always. You may be presented with a 300-yard shot at a buck in a midwestern grain field, or in one of the "green fields" of the South, just as you'd be faced with on the western prairie.

Western hunters typically use bolt-action rifles for muleys, topped with a scope which, more often than not, will be a variable 3X9. But that's not to say you must do likewise. It's far better to use the deer rifle you've used for years than to buy a "stereotyped" version that's "western." You'll find very few western hunters using semi-autos and single-shot rifles, but you might see a few carbines and pumps.

Because of the possibility of long-range shots, consider using a rifle capable of delivering a projectile with accuracy out to 300 yards or so. That distance is about maximum for most hunters. No one should shoot a deer much farther away unless he or she is expert at shooting long range.

I would, in every case, discourage a hunter from bringing out a rifle in .30/30 Win, .35 Rem, .444 Marlin, etc. These firearms are superb at (and were made for) very close shots. The ballistics of rifles such as these are terrible out at 150 yards and more, and simply can't be counted on to perform at long distances.

Unfortunately, many hunters who live in urban areas don't have a shooting range that offers tar-

gets much beyond 100 yards. Some offer 200-yard targets, and that's about it. Yet that hunter may be faced with a 300-yard shot when a muley buck offers an opportunity, and may fire away, hoping for the best, completely ignorant of what his bullet is doing.

It's okay to say you won't take any shots over 200 yards. I know plenty of hunters who say that, which is why many opt to use a short-range gun such as the .30/30. But what will you do with a firearm like that when the buck of your dreams is standing across a canyon 250 yards or more away? It's tempting to take a shot longer than we're confident in if a big buck presents himself. Even if we are indeed using a flat-shooting rifle, it's important to understand ballistics, knowing precisely where that bullet will hit at the range it's being fired at.

Prepare yourself for the long shot by getting permission to shoot in areas that offer distant yardages. An excellent way to practice is to hunt

woodchucks or other nuisance animals where you can set up in open country. Use the same gun you'll use on your deer hunt, and try all the shooting positions, including offhand, kneeling, sitting and prone.

When it comes down to drawing a bead on your buck, be sure you have a steady rest. Many deer have been missed because a firm rest wasn't used.

The choice of calibers is subject to endless debate. If it were up to me, I'd be perfectly happy with a .270, 7mm Mag, or a .30/06. Those are among the top three calibers in the West, but that's not to say that everything from a .25/06 up to a .338 isn't acceptable. In my opinion, the old reliables such as the Model 70 Winchester and Model 700 Remington, both bolt action rifles, are perfect for muleys. And if you want something with a little more punch, try one of the Weatherbys or the new Remington Ultra-Mags. If you have a tight budget in mind, try Remington's new 710, a bolt-action rifle fitted with a scope that retails for around $350. The .30/06 caliber would be my choice.

My first "western" rifle was a Winchester Model 70 in .30/06 caliber. With that rifle I took upwards of 60 or 70 muleys, and never had any misgivings.

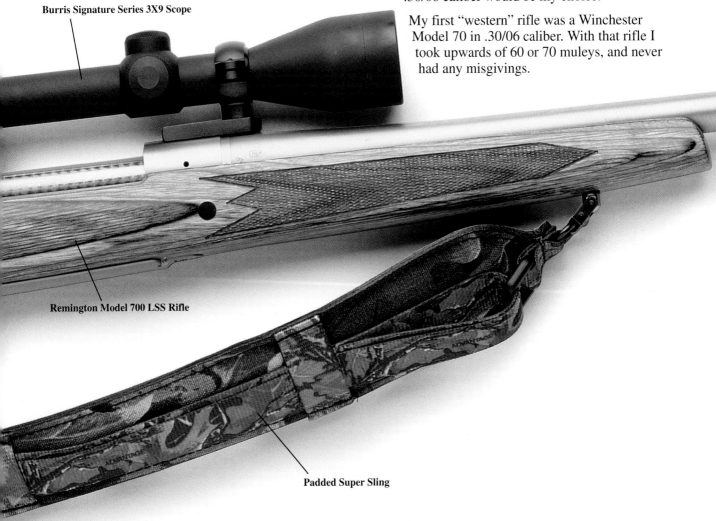

Burris Signature Series 3X9 Scope

Remington Model 700 LSS Rifle

Padded Super Sling

Recommended Rifle Calibers

TYPE OF CARTRIDGE (shown ⅔ actual size)	Muzzle Velocity (in fps*)	ENERGY (in foot-pounds)				TRAJECTORY (in inches above or below line of aim)				
		100 Yds.	200 Yds.	300 Yds.	400 Yds.	100 Yds.	150 Yds.	200 Yds.	300 Yds.	400 Yds.
.243 Winchester 100 Grain	2960	1615	1332	1089	882	+1.9	+1.6	0.0	-7.8	-22.6
.270 Winchester 130 Grain	3060	2225	1818	1472	1180	+1.8	+1.5	0.0	-7.4	-21.6
7mm Rem. Magnum 150 Grain	3110	2667	2196	1792	1448	+1.7	+1.5	0.0	-7.0	-20.5
.30-06 Springfield 150 Grain	2910	2281	1827	1445	1131	+2.1	+1.8	0.0	-8.5	-25.0
.300 Win. Magnum 180 Grain	2960	3011	2578	2196	1859	+1.9	+1.6	0.0	-7.3	-20.9

* Feet per second

The rifle was a pre-64 Featherweight version, and came equipped with a four-power scope with a dot reticule, and a sling.

Nowadays I still use a .30/06, but have become fond of other calibers as well. As I mentioned, a flat-shooting rifle is of paramount importance; the caliber is largely your choice. I'd stay away from the larger calibers and magnums simply because of the excess damage to meat. If you put a heavy bullet into the shoulders of a deer, count on losing one-fourth or more of the meat.

I've always considered that an adequate bullet for muleys should deliver at least 1,200 foot pounds of energy at 200 yards, which essentially translates to a .243. This caliber complies with the minimum caliber restrictions as set by law in many states. In Wyoming, where I live, for example, .23 is the minimum caliber size, effectively ruling out all the centerfire .22's.

While I could make a case for practically any firearm, the most important requirement is bullet placement. It doesn't matter if you're a handloader with the finest custom rifle ever made, it's up to you to hold the firearm steady and squeeze the trigger at the precise moment.

Bullets are, of course, another hot topic around the campfire. I believe that every bullet offered by major manufacturers today is capable of quickly and humanely killing a deer. Over the years, I've come back to the Remington Core-Lokt as my bullet of choice, and only because of habit. Those were the first bullets I used, and I gained confidence in them. However, I've had excellent results with Winchester Silvertips, Federal Trophy Bonded Bearclaws, and Noslers. Each bullet performs a bit differently, but each will get the job done.

I believe it's far better to quit fretting about the construction of your bullet, and to pay more attention to its delivery. Become intensely familiar with your rifle, gain confidence in it, and always use a rest of some sort.

A sling is a must in mule deer country, allowing you to carry the rifle over your shoulder, and helping you hold it steady if no rest is available.

What type of stock to buy? Not long ago, the only choice was wood, but today's synthetic models have proven popular and are becoming more common. These stocks are lighter than wood, and don't swell in wet weather, making them more accurate.

Stainless barrels are now in vogue, which allows less firearm maintenance, and a variety of muzzlebrakes are available to reduce recoil. Unfortunately, the muzzlebrake also increases the noise factor, becoming a serious contributor to hearing loss.

Nowadays many hunters are looking at lightweight rifles, guns that weigh 7 pounds or less. That's prudent thinking if you're planning on doing a lot of hiking, which is common in mule deer country that isn't laced with roads.

To repeat the advice of scores of hunting writers, familiarity with your firearm is of paramount importance. The style of the gun, caliber and choice of bullet are far less important than your ability to shoot it. That's the bottom line.

Muzzleloading

More and more mule deer hunters are taking to the woods these days with muzzleloaders, usually for different reasons than whitetail hunters in the East and Midwest. Whereas the latter often use muzzleloaders for safety reasons (hunting in crowded urban areas), western regulations are aimed at distributing hunting pressure.

In areas where modern firearms are allowed, plenty of hunters use muzzleloaders because of personal preference. The one-shot feature and relatively poor ballistics endear the muzzleloader to hunters wanting more of a challenge. They like getting closer to the quarry and knowing that their first shot will probably be the only one they'll get.

Muzzleloaders, also called black powder guns, are in themselves undergoing enormous technological advances. In 1985, Tony Knight, a Missouri hunter and retired railroad man, invented the "in-line" system that modernized muzzleloading and gave it a brand-new look.

Whatever you shoot, all muzzleloading firearms have two things in common: they offer one shot, and they're loaded from the muzzle.

Here are the basics: Powder is first put into the muzzle, over which a projectile is seated. Ignition is accomplished via a variety of techniques, each of them unique. When ignition occurs, regardless of the method, heat travels through a flash hole, ignites the powder and ejects the bullet down the barrel.

Most complicated is the flintlock, a rifle which is often considered the most traditional. This rifle has an external ignition system; a small amount of very fine powder is poured into the flash pan and is ignited when the flint or hammer strikes the steel, or frizzen, creating a spark. A small explosion sends heat into the gun via a flash hole, and the powder charge behind the projectile is then ignited, sending the bullet or ball down the barrel. Obviously a number of events must perfectly occur in order for the gun to fire properly.

A percussion caplock works in similar fashion. Instead of the flash pan, a cap is placed on a nipple. When struck by the hammer, the cap explodes and sends heat through the flash hole.

The in-line system is the modern version, and, as the name implies, has all the firing components – striker, cap, nipple, flash hole and powder, all in a straight line. The Knight Disc rifle goes a step further and

"FFFFg"

Black Powder Grades
(shown 2 ¼ times actual size)

"FFFg"

"FFg"

"Fg"

uses a shotgun primer instead of a percussion cap, resulting in far more reliability.

The basic propellants are standard black powder, or Pyrodex, a black powder substitute, though there are a few others. Many hunters these days have turned to Pyrodex because it's more stable and safer, and doesn't leave as much residue in the barrel as black powder does; thus the gun requires less cleaning. There are various grades of black powder, starting at FFFFg, the finest, to Fg, the coarsest. Flintlock pans perform best when loaded the finest, while the Fg works best in shotguns. Most mule deer hunters will use FFg in their rifles. Pyrodex comes in several grades, though RS is the norm for muzzle-loaders used by deer hunters. Some hunters are using Pyrodex pellets these days, which basically are 30- or 50-grain cylinders less than an inch long that are easily popped into the barrel, thus eliminating the requirement of measuring and dumping in loose powder.

When determining the best load for your rifle, it's a good idea to consult with an expert who can offer solid advice. Or you can experiment yourself, starting with 90 grains or so, and working different loads until you find the one that works best for you. Typically, 100 grains is most common, but some guns perform best with more or less. To help in getting off a more timely second shot, consider a quickload. These are small tubes about 3 inches long that hold the powder in one end and a projectile in the other. If your muley gives you a chance for a second shot, you won't need to search for powder and projectile; both will be handy in the quickload.

Projectiles come in three basic designs: the round ball, conical bullet and sabot. The latter is simply a bullet encased in a plastic sleeve. Of the three, the round ball is the worst performer; the sabot the best. Though there are a variety of projectiles, most common in round ball weights are 180 grains in .50 caliber and 215 grains in .54 caliber. The conical bullet typically is 385 grains in .50 caliber to 425 grains in .54 caliber. Sabot bullets vary from 180 grains to 325 grains.

Loading the firearm involves placing the projectile in the muzzle once the appropriate amount of powder has been added. A tool called a short start assists in initially pushing the projectile in, and a ramrod is then used to seat the bullet or ball firmly against the powder. The ramrod is carried under the barrel, where it slides into rings.

Because muzzleloading firearms foul with every shot, whether you're using black powder or Pyrodex, you need to clean the gun thoroughly. Of course, if you're hunting and need a quick second or even third shot, you won't have time to do so. To clean the gun, you can't simply run a patch through the barrel, as you do with a modern firearm. It must be taken apart and cleaned, and when finished, lubricating oils should be applied. If you're shooting at a range where you have time between shots, run a clean patch down the barrel each time you shoot.

There seem to be two separate types of black powder hunters, the traditionalists and the modern hunters. The former typically wear buckskins, use flintlocks or caplocks, and are more into the old-fashioned accouterments used by frontiersmen. The modern hunters tend to wear camo and shoot in-line guns, though some prefer the more traditional firearms. Unfortunately, there are members of each group who are at odds with the other. Some traditionalists don't like the idea of hunters using the modern in-lines, especially if they're equipped with scopes. Many feel that the high-tech guns diminish the romance of muzzleloader hunting. Modern hunters, on the other hand, sometimes complain that the traditionalists shoot guns that are inherently more inaccurate; than modern guns thus more animals are wounded. This is unfortunate because divisiveness is the last thing we need in our sport.

Pyrodex pellets
(Shown 2 ¼ times actual size)

Because of all the gear required, a "possibles bag," usually made from leather, carries all the equipment needed to fire and care for the firearm. Some of these bags have dangling buckskin fronds, some are beautifully beaded, and many are homemade.

Why do mule deer hunters need to use muzzleloaders in the first place? There are two reasons; one is strictly to hunt quality units offering bigger bucks as well as the opportunity for more solitude and quiet when we hunt. Many states have muzzleloader-only seasons, or special units available to muzzleloader hunters. Permits are offered on a quota in most states, and a lottery draw is required to obtain a tag. The other reason is simply the challenge of using a one-shot firearm as well as the pleasure of using the primitive gun, whether it's a traditional or in-line gun. The need to get closer to the quarry holds special appeal for many folks. I use a muzzleloader for both reasons. Some of my fondest memories involve several black powder mule deer hunts in a Utah primitive area, where you'd be lucky to see two or three hunters in a day. During the general firearms season, there would be an army of hunters in the area. That's one of the reasons that I'll head for mule deer country with my muzzleloader as often as I can.

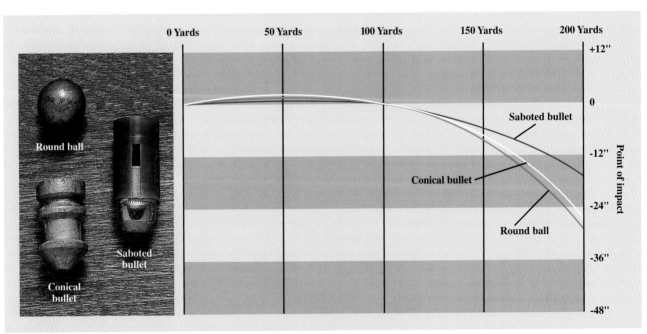

BULLET TRAJECTORY for saboted bullets is flatter than that of conicals and round balls. As the illustration above shows, a saboted bullet sighted in at 100 yards hits only 1½ inches high at 50 yards and 6 inches low at 150 yards.

Bowhunting

It's my opinion that bowhunting for mule deer is the greatest archery challenge in the country, and I'm including whitetails, elk and other big-game animals. Consider this: most whitetail bowhunters are in a treestand, often overlooking a line of scrapes or rubs. Whitetails readily come to calls and rattling if the season is correct. Elk are bowhunted during the rut when they can be called within range with a bugle or cow call. Antelope can be decoyed or effectively hunted around waterholes. A mule deer, on the other hand, does not respond well to calling or rattling, it doesn't make scrapes, its rubs are helter skelter and seldom consistent, and it's tough to hunt from a treestand over much of its range.

I think the biggest challenge in bowhunting big game is to spot and stalk a muley buck, one on one, in the typical brushy cover where it lives. Trying to ease in close to a buck on foot, with all the intervening foliage, is a major effort, and one that very few hunters can accomplish.

Bowhunting seasons for mule deer may vary enormously with the state being hunted, from mid-August to December. Because of these variations, the technique will depend on the season being hunted. In August, for example, hunters may set up around waterholes, or opt to stillhunt in very high elevations where deer are summering. In December, archers will want to take advantage of the rut and hunt where plenty of does are present.

EQUIPMENT FOR BOWHUNTING

By far the majority of mule deer hunters will use a compound bow, but it wasn't that way a few

decades ago when compounds just came on the scene. Prior to that, recurves were most popular, replacing the traditional longbows. The latter is the most challenging to shoot, offering no mechanical advantages through design or gadgets. Many longbows are still made out of by custom shops or are homemade. The recurve is normally constructed of laminated wood or fiberglass, and has double-flexed limbs.

The compound bow has achieved so much acclaim primarily because of its ease to shoot and accuracy. There are dozens of designs on the market, each of them having a unique system of cams and pulleys, and limbs typically constructed of molded or laminated fiberglass. The most important feature of the compound that makes it exclusively unique is its let-off ability, which reduces the draw weight at full draw as much as 50 to 80 percent. This allows you to draw back the string and have a fraction of the weight to hold back, since the bow mechanisms take up the brunt of the draw weight. Let's say you have a compound bow with a 60-pound draw weight and an 80 percent let-off rate. Since 80 percent of 60 is 48, the difference is 12 pounds, which you hold at full draw. This means that you can hold the string back at full draw far longer than you could a recurve or long bow. If a deer is meandering through brush, for example, and is about to walk through an opening, you can draw back and hold the string for several seconds, until the animal presents the appropriate

target. Besides this very nice option, the compound bow also shoots the arrow faster, which means it has a flatter trajectory and more energy downrange.

There are two types of archers – those who shoot instinctively and those who use sights. The instinctive shooter lines up the target with nothing more than his eye, and depends on plenty of practice to achieve accuracy. The sight-shooter has dozens of different types of sights to choose from, and typically lines up a peep sight on the string when at full draw with the corresponding pin above the arrow rest. Each pin represents a different distance. The critical factor here is knowing precisely the range of the deer, which often foils even the best shooters, though a number of range-finder devices are now available to resolve this problem.

Arrows are far different than they were just a few decades ago. The new carbon and aluminum arrows have largely replaced the wooden and fiberglass arrows, offering far more uniformity and consistency. Carbon arrows are lighter and faster than aluminum, but the latter are preferred by many hunters because they're heavier and penetrate more readily. Many hunters are using a mechanical release, which eliminates the inherent inaccuracy when releasing with your fingers.

When buying arrows, it's a good idea to purchase them from a archery proshop where experts can help you select those that are best suited for your bow.

Effects of Slope on Trajectory

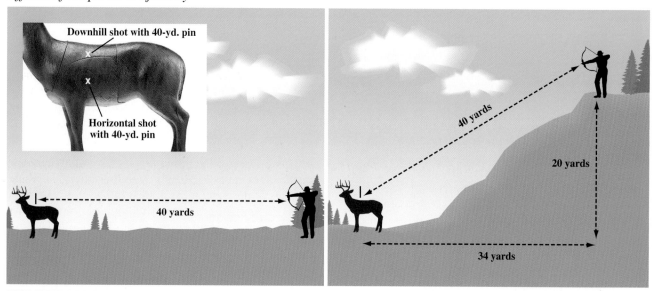

THE EFFECTS OF SLOPE on trajectory can be explained by the physics of gravity. Gravity exerts its influence only against the horizontal distance of an arrow's flight. When you shoot horizontally at a target 40 yards away (left), gravity exerts its influence for a full 40 yards, and the arrow's drop follows expectations. But when you shoot downhill (right) or uphill at a target 40 yards away, the horizontal distance can actually be much less, as shown above. In this situation, if you shoot using the 40-yard sight pin, your arrow will hit high on the target (inset), since it has not had time to complete its normal trajectory drop for 40 horizontal yards.

The same is true with all other gear, from bows to sights and other items. Personnel in those stores are usually experts, and can help you through the process of determining the right gear for you. They'll measure your draw length and help you decide on a bow with a draw weight that is appropriate for your needs. Many pro-shops have indoor ranges where you can practice with different equipment until you find what works best for you. Friendly employees will actually show you how to shoot, from finding and using your anchor point to a myriad of other tips that will make you a more accurate shooter.

Fletching was once exclusively feathers; nowadays it can be feathers or plastic, and most often is the latter. The function of the fletching is to stabilize the arrow in flight and help it rotate.

The nock is the plastic tip that holds the groove where the string lies. Most hunters prefer brightly colored nocks and fletching, allowing the arrow to be more visible in flight. This is essential in determining the trajectory of the arrow and seeing if it hit the target area. Bright fletching also helps the hunter locate arrows after the shot.

The broadhead rounds out the last of the arrow components. This is often called the most important part of the arrow, but in reality everything must work perfectly or the arrow won't hit the target where the broadhead then performs its function. Broadheads must be matched to the arrow shaft, and they must be absolutely razor-sharp. There's a great variety on the market, and they have different shapes and blades. Some blades are detachable and replaceable, and are becoming more popular among bowhunters. It's important that the broadheads you use are of the same exact weight as the field tips that you use when you practice. In fact, some bowhunters actually practice exclusively with broadheads.

Every hunter is aware of the need to practice, regardless of the way he or she chooses to hunt. But it's incumbent on the bowhunter to practice relentlessly, until accuracy is the norm and not the exception. It's commonly advised among bowhunters that one should practice an hour every day 2 or 3 months prior to hunting season. That's good advice, but not within the busy schedule of many hunters. Nonetheless, the more you can practice, the better.

Because muleys are most often hunted from ground level, and at many angles, it's smart to practice shooting from a variety of positions. When it's time to take the shot, be certain that your arrow penetrates the lungs. Aim just at the crease of the shoulder, and take the shot when the deer is distracted, if you can. Never aim at the neck because of the possibility of missing

---

Common Bowhunting Errors

• Being spotted by quarry. A muley may see you if your camo apparel isn't adequate, or, more importantly, if he sees you draw. Never pull the string back until the deer's eyes are momentarily screened by brush or trees. Wait until he moves behind vegetation before drawing, and always have your bow properly positioned long before the shot. Nock the arrow prior to the point where the deer might see you, and be ready for the shot.

• Noise. A bow can be unwieldy in cover, and can make noise that will easily betray your position. When you set up in an area, be sure that the brush close by is removed or cut back so you can swing your bow easily without striking brush and making unnecessary sounds that will alert deer.

• Not being ready. Always have an arrow nocked and ready if you anticipate a shot. Too many hunters wait until the last minute, and then it's too late because the quarry is close and any movement on the part of the hunter will be a dead give-away.

• Poor shooting lanes. If you have time and are watching trails, cut shooting lanes in the brush. Try to figure where deer will approach, and anticipate several options. Carry small clippers to cut brush and twigs.

• Buck fever. There's no cure for this malady, but you can make an effort to concentrate as mightily as you can, remembering the precise movements you must make. Think intently about a smooth draw, and line up the quarry as precisely as you can with the sights you're using.

---

the spine and striking the muscle. Avoid taking a shot if there's a remote chance that the arrow will hit a branch or twig between you and the deer. If an obstacle is struck, your arrow will be instantly aborted, and will fall harmlessly away from the target.

Because of the need to remain as still and invisible as possible, camouflage clothing is a must. There are dozens of designs on the market today, and most will work in mule deer country, though it's a good idea to choose a pattern that closely resembles the landscape you'll be hunting in. Face paint is used widely, but I prefer a face mask, which performs the same function and doesn't require the messy chore of applying and removing paint. Scents that keep human odor down are often used by hunters, as well as the new high-tech clothing that keeps scent to a minimum.

Hunting Optics

Mule deer country is a natural for optics because of the typical openness and long-range visibility. Binoculars and a scoped rifle are standard fare in the West, and astute hunters carry a spotting scope as well.

It's human nature to look for bargains when we shop for anything, including hunting gear, but optics should never be considered because of their low cost. I'm not suggesting you shell out a handsome four-digit amount for European optics. If you can, you won't regret the purchase, but some very affordable models are quite satisfactory for mule deer hunting.

BINOCULARS

Binoculars are important for two reasons: safety and smart hunting. Why safety, you ask? Consider this: Let's say you're hunting with a scoped rifle and carrying no binoculars. You see something move in the brush, or see a suspicious shape that you can't identify. Your natural reaction might be to shoulder the rifle and look through your scope to check it out. That's a serious error. Suppose that object turned out to be another hunter? You'd be aiming your rifle at a human being. I once looked at the wrong end of a distant loaded rifle and I can tell you it was a horrible experience. Luckily the other hunter who was aiming his rifle at me decided I wasn't fair game.

Using binoculars to help you locate game and evaluate it is a routine aspect of hunting. I believe binoculars are as important on a hunt as your rifle, even if you're hunting blacktails in the thickest rain forest on the continent. There will always come a time when you'll need to look at something with binoculars, regardless of the cover.

Before deciding on the binoculars for you, it's a good idea to know something about the basics. There are two binocular designs, the porro prism and roof prism. The porro is the style that has an offset profile of both tubes, while the roof prism has straight parallel tubes. The roof prism has actually been around for 50 years or more, but has just come into popularity over the last 15 or 20 years. An advantage is less weight and bulk – two factors important to hunters who hike in rough country.

Both styles have a pair of prismatic-erecting telescopes that appear as one when placed to the eyes. Each tube will move so that it fits the eyes of the observer. In the case of hunters who wear eyeglasses, the tube will be fitted with a device that will allow the binoculars to be held closer to the eyes. A rubber ring or movable extension device positions the tubes accordingly.

When looking into binoculars, be aware that one of the tubes (almost always the right tube) will have a separate focus ring or lever. This insures that your eyes will be properly adjusted to the binoculars. To make the adjustment, put the glasses to your face, close your left eye, and turn the focus ring until the object you're looking at is in focus. Then, with both eyes open, use the general focus ring, which is between the tubes, to adjust the focus for the distance you're looking at. If you're looking at something 75 yards away, for example, you'll focus for that distance, but if you then look at something 200 yards away, you'll need to turn the ring until the object comes into focus.

On every set of binoculars you'll see two sets of figures. The first is the magnifying power, and the second is the diameter of the objective lens in millimeters. The ocular lens is the one closest to the eye, while the objective lens is farthest away. Let's say your binoculars are 10X50s. That means your glasses have a magnification (or power) of 10, and the objective lens is 50 millimeters in diameter. Be aware that the higher-power glasses are harder to steady because the greatly magnified image bounces around more.

It's important to know that binoculars with large objective lenses are best when light conditions are poor. Think of it this way: a big window lets in more light than a small window; thus glasses with 50mm objective lenses are far better than binoculars with 25 or 30mm objective lenses if the light is low, such as early morning or late afternoon. There's an interesting term called the "twilight factor," which is a rating that indicates the effectiveness of binoculars when the light is poor. To get the twilight factor, you simply multiply the power by the size of the objective lens, and then take the square root of that number.

The higher the number, the more light enters the tubes, and the better you can see during those magic minutes when shooting light begins and ends each day.

Besides having the capability of seeing images early and late, binoculars should have a crisp focus, not just to allow you to see intricate details, but to probe into the shade and shadows on distant slopes to spot a piece of the quarry that might otherwise be hidden from view.

Your binoculars should be waterproof for obvious reasons. If you intend on hiking a great deal, consider lightweight glasses, though you'll need to go with the lower power in order to do so. Remember that the higher magnification glasses are always the heaviest. To cope with heavy glasses, consider one of the harness straps that clip on and keep your binoculars snugged up to your chest. They won't be swinging side to side or banging into you as you walk, hike or ride horseback.

No matter how good your binoculars are, they'll be worthless unless you know how to use them. In fairly open terrain, you can use them all day long, looking for deer in and around cover. Deer aren't always bedded continuously during the day, but may be temporarily up on their feet, nibbling here and there or simply changing locations. If it's a hot, bright day, deer may move with the shade. I once observed a buck change bedding locations three times over the course of 4 hours because he apparently didn't want to lie in the direct sunlight. Each time he got up to seek a shaded spot he'd nibble on browse for a

minute or two and then bed down. Of course, it's far easier to spot a buck standing than one lying down.

Use your binoculars continuously as soon as you get to your hunting area in the morning, even if it's before shooting hours. The same is true late in the afternoon. Those precious minutes before sunrise and after sunset are the periods that muleys are most active, and that's when you need to look for them.

When you glass, find a comfortable position so you won't be tempted to leave sooner than you might. Look in the shaded areas, in and around pockets of brush, and let your eyes penetrate the vegetation, always looking for the telltale clue that might betray a deer. Too many hunters make a cursory look and give up before really giving the area a thorough look.

RIFLE SCOPES

Every now and then you'll see a mule deer hunter using an open-sighted rifle, but the vast majority use scopes. The open nature of muley country and the chance for long shots makes a scope practical and essentially mandatory.

Scopes come in all sorts of powers and different-sized objective lenses, and many have bells and whistles to help you make a long shot by offering compensation options.

For example, if you line up a distant deer with lines or circles in the scope, the appropriate elevation can be made. That's a nice idea on paper, but, in my opinion, next to worthless when it comes to reality. Any time you are required to think before taking a shot, you are wasting precious seconds that might cause the quarry to flee. I believe a "clean" scope with no fancy images is far better; you simply make a judgment call as to yardage and take the shot. Besides, if an animal is so far out that you must use a guide to help you shoot, it's probably too far out anyway.

A few years ago, laser rangefinders made their way into hunting camps. These look like binoculars, but have twin tubes on one end and a single tube at the other. You simply look through the tubes, aim at the target and push a button. A digital readout within the instrument appears and tells you exactly how far away the target is. The big disadvantage is the extra weight and additional gadget to carry around your neck.

As in binoculars, the lens of the rifle scope closest to your eye is

Brunton 7X42 Binoculars

the ocular lens, the one farthest is the objective. Scopes may be fixed, having a single power, or variable, having a range of powers. The 3X9 is the most common variable scope, though there are many other possibilities. Some hunters will use the higher power to see details on a distant deer, and then turn to lower power for the shot. It's far better to leave the power on one setting and use your binoculars if you need more magnification. In some cheaper scopes, the bullet's point of impact may change depending on the power. For example, if you sight the rifle in with the scope on 9 power, the shot may be profoundly off if you dial down to 3 or 4 power. Always check your scope out on the range to be sure it isn't doing this. My first scope was an old Weaver 4-power that I used for 20 years. I got along perfectly fine with it on hundreds of mule deer hunts and never found it to be lacking.

The reticle in a scope is the image that you line up on the target, such as standard crosshairs, a dot in the center of the crosshairs, a post, or many other combinations. There are literally dozens of reticules; I prefer a crosshair with a small dot. The dot helps me line up the sights in poor light, such as the first or last minutes of shooting hours on a cloudy day.

A scope must be absolutely waterproof. This is the only optical item that truly must have the waterproof feature, because your shot will be guided by the scope. If your buck shows up and you can't see it because your scope is fogged, the gun is worthless.

Some scopes are mounted very high so you can see the open sights under them if necessary. Most hunters, however, use convienient flip-up scope covers to keep the lenses clear.

Every scope has two adjustment rings; the one on top allows for elevation, the one on the side for windage. To make the adjustment, simply turn the dial in the direction as indicated by the arrow. Note the number of clicks required to sight in properly. This information may or may not be on the scope; if not, you should find it in the manual.

SPOTTING SCOPES

Not long ago, spotting scopes were used only by outfitters, guides and very serious hunters. They were bulky and heavy, but today there are a number of lightweight, compact versions available. The single-tube scope offers much higher magnification than binoculars, and may be either fixed or variable. The fixed scopes are generally 20 or 30 power, but the variables may go from 15 to 50 power or more.

Spotting scopes are valuable when regulations require a legal buck to have a minimum number of antler points, especially if the brow tine counts as a point (brow tines can be extremely short and hard to see). In that case, you'll need to see details of the antler configuration if the buck is questionable and if he'll hold still long enough for you to make the evaluation. The smaller spotting scopes will fit nicely in a backpack, along with a tripod that is also collapsible and lightweight. A tripod is a must; it's virtually impossible to steady a spotting scope on a log, rock, or tree branch to where it can be functional.

Clothing

Hunting mule deer can occur during any weather extreme, depending on when and where you hunt. I've hunted them from -25°F in late November to 100° plus in late August. Obviously, it's essential to be properly attired in order to maintain some degree of comfort, as well as to avoid the very serious consequences of heat stroke or hypothermia. There's always the chance, too, of several weather extremes in a single day, given the ever-changing nature of weather in the mountain country.

If you're driving to the hunt you'll be able to toss in all sorts of clothing, but if you're flying you'll need to keep your baggage within certain weight restrictions. A horseback hunt with an outfitter might require you to cut back even more.

Don't be lulled into a false sense of security that a September hunt will be warm and dry, even if you checked the forecast on the Internet! Expect the worst, especially if you're hunting in the mountains. A low-elevation hunt in sagebrush or the desert might also be dealt some severe weather in the form of extensive rainfall and even snow.

Remember that the higher you go in elevation, the colder the temperature and the more possibility of rain or snow. Typically, early to mid-October weather can be blue sky and balmy, with more chance of snow and colder temperatures as the month progresses. In November, anything goes, and the weather can change from summer to winter in a matter of hours. In the early 90s I was headed on a mule deer hunt in Montana for the opener, which was in late October. On this hunt we planned on taking a boat across a reservoir and hunting a place accessible only by water. A few days prior to the hunt, the temperature dipped to -20°F and hung in for days. The bay where we hoped to launch was frozen tight, foiling our hunt plans. That was one of the coldest autumns on record, and many hunters were woefully unprepared for the bitterly cold temperatures.

As a rule of thumb, purchase garments that are manufactured by reputable companies, and don't fall for cheap prices. Quality clothing can be fairly expensive, but it will be well worth the price and will last a long time if you properly take care of it. Be sure you follow laundering instructions on the garment before attempting to wash it.

COATS AND PANTS

Most western states require hunter orange during firearms seasons, the amount and type depending on the state you're hunting. In some, you must wear a minimum number of square inches, which is normally satisfied by a vest. A hunter orange cap may or may not be required, and in some states you must wear only solid hunter orange rather than a camo pattern. In states that don't require orange, I believe it's a good idea to wear it anyway for safety reasons. Some hunters resist wearing orange because they think it spooks deer. I don't believe that's the case, having been approached by whitetails and muleys alike when wearing it. I believe movement and the human form put deer at alert.

It's not uncommon for some hunters to buy a high-quality hunting jacket in camo pattern, and then top it off with a cheap hunter orange vest to satisfy the legal requirement. That's a mistake; the vest could cost you a fine buck because the vest is noisy in the brush. Give as much thought to buying "quiet" orange outerwear as you do to basic clothing.

If you're hunting deer in the desert or sagebrush and the weather is expected to be hot and dry, toss an extra shirt in your daypack anyway. It can chill off quickly once the sun goes down and you'll be glad you had it along. In the mountains, however, prepare for the worst. Keep an extra woolen shirt and compact rainsuit in your daypack. Rather than wearing a single heavy, bulky jacket, consider the layered effect, where you can take off or add garments as the weather changes.

Raingear isn't always what it's cracked up to be. I've jumped through plenty of hoops, trying to find just the right material that works. Most of it doesn't, and I always learn the hard way. The good news is that it's more apt to snow than rain in mule deer country, and snow is far easier to deal with. Gore-tex is normally a good choice for outer rainwear, and has been around for many years. I'm a big fan of wool, and have been using it as long as I can remember. I've found that it works well except in extended downpours when the bottom falls out of the sky for several hours or days, and I've had bad experiences with wool in extremely strong windstorms. When choosing raingear, I'm adamant about the hood being permanently attached to the jacket rather than being attached by buttons or fasteners. The latter always seem to get disconnected, and water easily seeps in.

Flannel or cotton is the worst fabric to wear. It quickly gets wet and stays wet for a long time. Blue jeans are the garment of choice for many western hunters, including me, but they're terrible in snow, rain and cold weather.

Down is often considered the ultimate filler, because it provides plenty of warmth. But beware in wet weather. It becomes totally worthless, sopping up water like a sponge, and is extremely difficult to dry. There are all sorts of synthetic fillers on the market that are far superior to down in bad weather. But I really like down in very cold, dry weather. A good shell will protect it from snow, and you'll be snug and warm as long as no moisture gets in. I like the idea of down's source. After all, anything that's made of the under-feathers of a goose has to be good. I feel the same about wool. But it's a fact that manmade materials often excel under extremely wet and windy situations.

UNDERWEAR

In very cold weather, undergarments are a must. I like chloropropylene longjohns best, but there are excellent garments made from polypropylene and silk. It's a good idea to wear longjohn bottoms when you're going on an extended horseback ride, even in warm weather, since they'll prevent chafing and skin irritation.

No undergarments will be effective if you must be still for a long period of time after they become wet from perspiration. You'll be okay as long as you're exercising – it's the stopping that makes you uncomfortable. You may not have an option of preventing perspiration when you're chasing muleys around the mountains. When you feel yourself heating up, take off a layer and stow in it your daypack. Put it back on if you stop to glass and begin to chill down.

HATS

Practically everyone wears a hat while hunting, but some are worthless in bad weather, especially the inexpensive baseball caps that are so common. Since much heat is lost through the head, wear a good sturdy hat that has ear muffs. I like a heavy-duty woolen watch cap that pulls down over my ears, but it sits in my daypack if I'm facing the morning or evening sun. Since the watch cap has no bill, it doesn't shade the bright rays. If you're dealing with strong winds, wear a ski mask or balaclava that protects your face. I can remember many frigid mule deer hunts when I would have paid a healthy fee to have some kind of face protection. Rosy, red cheeks might be the "look" of an outdoorsman, but they can hurt!

Gloves

No one in his or her right mind will go afield on a cold day without gloves, but it's not uncommon for hands to get cold. This varies with each individual, since extremities can get colder with some people than others. If you have a problem with cold hands, buy high-quality gloves, and consider a pair slightly larger than your fit so you can insert a handwarmer packet in each. Those little items are amazing and work wonders when you're really cold. If you intend to sit for a period of time, use bulky mittens or even a muff, but be prepared to get them off quickly if you need to take a quick shot. I will not use a gloved trigger finger, so I choose gloves that have a slit where you can poke your finger out and make skin contact with the trigger.

Boots

Boots are a vital component of your apparel, but too few people pay attention to buying adequate boots and breaking them in properly. There is no such thing as a boot for all occasions. Boots must be matched for the weather, amount and degree of use, and the terrain. If you hunt mule deer in the desert in September, for example, you'll likely want lightweight boots that are ankle-high. On the other hand, if you're hunting in 2 feet of powder snow in late November, you'll obviously need higher boots that are well insulated and waterproof. My favorite boots for snow and cold are the type that have leather on the upper part and rubber on the bottom. Felt innersoles that easily slide in and out can be easily dried in the evenings. Bring along a replacement pair in case your regular ones don't dry overnight.

Irish Setter Expeditions

Most importantly, break your boots in before your hunt. Wear them for several weeks if you can, around the house or even at work. The last thing you want on your mule deer hunt is to have feet that hurt because your boots are too stiff or ill-fitting. If your feet don't work, you'll be demoralized, and physically incapable of getting around. That could spell the difference between success or failure.

When buying boots, you may notice that there's a temperature rating that goes along with them. For example, many boots are rated at 50 or even 75 degrees below zero. Don't believe it! Companies should be ashamed of themselves for listing those ratings, because they are totally meaningless. You can freeze your toes at 5 below while wearing boots rated at 75 below. Those ratings reflect the boot's capabilities when you're at full exercise, such as jogging or running behind a dogsled, and certainly not when sitting on a windy ridgetop or in a frigid tree stand, or even on a horse.

The soles under your boots are important, but few people understand how they function. Basically they're designed to grip uneven or frozen surfaces. I'm sold on the air-bob design, which works on every surface imaginable. Air bobs are small, round-shaped buttons that are strategically placed on the sole, offering outstanding traction. Most major boot companies offer these soles.

Socks

Quality socks are a must if you want comfortable feet during your hunt. Bring a fresh pair for each day, though if you're in a backcountry camp you might need to cut back. A solution is to wash soiled socks in a pan of warm water and soap, hang them to dry, and use them when required. In cold weather I wear a polypropylene sock topped with a heavy woolen sock.

Accessories

The nature of mule deer country lends itself to plenty of walking and hiking, unless you're unwilling or incapable of putting much distance between yourself and your vehicle. A roomy daypack gets my vote as being the ultimate means of carrying all the gear you'll need. A fanny pack will work if you anticipate a short hike, and you aren't worried about foul weather. In the case of bad weather, you won't be able to stow extra garments in a fanny pack as you would a daypack. The fanny pack is preferred by hunters who have back problems, because the load is supported by the hips and waist rather than the back.

DAYPACKS. The daypack was undoubtedly named because it carries enough gear for a day. It might better be termed simply a backpack, because it could indeed carry more than a day's gear if you so desire. Some daypacks are constructed so you can attach a sleeping bag, small tent, canteen and other items for an overnight trip.

There's a danger in making a decision to forego a pack if we have expectations of making only a short hike from the vehicle – and the short hike turns into

an all-day trek. I've done that more than once, and most of the time regretted leaving my pack behind. A typical scenario goes like this: you spot a likely-looking track in fresh snow, decide to follow for a few hundred yards to see where it's headed, and tell yourself that you'll return to your vehicle for your pack if you decide to make a long hike. But you begin following, and are so intense that you keep going until at some point you're far enough from the rig that you say to heck with it and continue without your pack. So there you are, with just light clothing, your rifle and binoculars, and no flashlights, extra clothing or other gear you might need. Perhaps even your knife is in the pack. To avoid this problem, always assume you're going on a marathon hike and take your pack with you every time you leave the vehicle, even if you're positive you'll only be gone for 10 minutes. Remember Murphy's Law.

When purchasing a pack, consider comfort first. If you can, try different packs on to see which offers the best fit. Be sure it rides properly on your back, has shoulder straps that are sufficiently wide, and has a waist strap that allows the pack to fit snugly around your middle. Of course, it's not possible to try on packs if you order from a catalog. The size depends on how much gear you intend to stow, which then depends on the kind of hunting you like to do. Packs have many compartments, side pockets, loops, straps, cords, and all sorts of ways to hold gear. Look them all over to determine what you'll really need and what's unnecessary. Be sure the pack is waterproof. Many are not. Obviously, you don't want your gear to get wet. Some packs can be converted so you can carry out a considerable amount of meat, and are lined with protective plastic. You'll also need to decide if you want a camo or hunter orange pack. If you bowhunt, you'll no doubt opt for the camo version. I use an orange pack simply for safety reasons. Then too, many western states require that you wear so many inches of hunter orange apparel. It makes no sense (and it might be illegal) to cover your upper torso with a camo pack even though you have hunter orange beneath.

When I think I might be hauling a muley out piece by piece, I'll bring along a few garbage bags to hold the meat so it won't soil the pack. However – and this is an important point – never put meat in plastic unless it's thoroughly chilled. If you must move warm meat, wrap it with several layers of cheesecloth, or better yet, put it in a heavy-duty reusable cloth bag made especially for that purpose. When soiled, bags can be washed in a washing machine and used over and over.

KNIVES. A knife is mandatory, of course. I like a fold-back knife that I use for field-dressing, and I also carry a fold-back fillet knife in my pack to bone and slice meat. This long-bladed knife is flexible, allowing me to cut tightly around bones. A sharpener is necessary to keep your knife blade honed. Another item seen more these days are disposable rubber gloves that protect you from diseases and parasites carried by deer, and also keep your hands cleaner. One company makes a two-set package – loose-fitting plastic gloves that extend up your arms to your shoulders, overtopped with tight-fitting gloves that cover your hands. This set keeps your sleeves from getting soiled during the dressing process. There's no need to carry a saw if you decide to dismantle your mule deer for the trip out of the woods. Simply use your knife and cut the quarters off the carcass at the joints, then slice the meat off the backstraps, flanks, and neck, and then remove the tenderloins. Or you can bone the entire carcass on the spot.

ROPE. Rope will come in handy for a number of uses, including hanging a carcass in a tree, dragging a deer, tying the front legs around the head before dragging, and other uses. When moving a deer that must be dragged, I like a special harness or drag system made exclusively for that purpose. They are typically designed with shoulder straps that allow you to pull with the upper torso rather than just your arms.

OPTICS. Optics (pg. 47) are a big part of my hunting strategies; I'd be lost without my binoculars, and most of the time I'll carry a lightweight, compact spotting scope in my pack. I wear the binoculars around my neck, secured with flexible straps that keep them from bouncing around when I hike in rough terrain or ride a horse.

COMPASS AND GPS. I seldom go anywhere without a compass, even if I think I'll be taking a short hike from the truck. And a map is always with me if I'm in unfamiliar country. I don't care much for a GPS, though I know lots of folks who use them. These units pinpoint your location by triangulating off three satellites and are practically infallible. But, in my opinion, anything that uses batteries is suspect. If you use a GPS, always have a compass as a backup.

EXTRA CLOTHING. I like to carry an extra shirt in my daypack as well as a very lightweight poncho, in the event of unexpected bad weather. A compact space blanket is welcome if I'm sitting in a stiff wind, since it will deflect much of the breeze, and becomes an important emergency item if I'm forced to overnight. Gloves and a wool hat are also part of my extra clothing.

KEEP SAFE. I carry a survival kit that contains waterproof matches, signaling mirror, whistle, and other items, as well as a small first aid kit. At least two flashlights are in my possession, no matter what time of day I'm hunting, along with an extra pack of fresh batteries. I use the small flashlights that take AA batteries.

FOOD AND WATER. Trail food is always welcome. I make up my own, mixing a variety of nuts, raisins, sunflower seeds, M&M's, dried bananas and other fruits that I dry myself. I also carry a small bag of hard candy.

A canteen slips into a holster on my belt, and if I'm hunting in grizzly country, I'll carry a canister of bear spray, also on a belt holster. I might also carry a small water filtration kit if I think I might need more water than my canteen will supply.

ORANGE FLAGGING. Orange flagging is a must. I'll use it to mark a route in or out from a downed deer, or for a variety of other uses. If I'm trailing a wounded deer, I'll carefully flag the trail, and I might use flagging to denote a precise spot on a ridge that I want to return to. In every case, I remove the flagging when I leave.

CAMERA. A small, compact point-and-shoot camera along with three or four rolls of film round out my accessories list. I like to chronicle my hunts by taking pictures of scenes, as well as an animal I've taken.

Keep your pack as light as possible by choosing only light, essential items. If in doubt, test any of the items if they're new and you aren't familiar with them.

Planning a Mule Deer Hunt

Where to Hunt Mule Deer

Knowing where to hunt muleys can be a major dilemma if you've never been west before, and even more of a problem if you don't know anyone who can share information with you.

As with most other western big-game species, the ability to simply get a deer tag may be one of the most difficult aspects of planning your hunt. Very few states nowadays offer across-the-counter tags to nonresidents, and in some states, even residents must apply for a tag.

The very first part of the planning process is selecting a state. This decision is based on your personal preference from things you've read and heard about a particular state, or perhaps having a friend that will hunt with you in a certain state, or the ability to get a tag. Another decision is whether you'll hunt on your own or hire an outfitter. Of course, the latter option eliminates all the guesswork. Once you have a tag, the outfitter will take care of all the details. For the purpose of this chapter, we'll assume you're not hunting with an outfitter.

Obviously, before you can select a state and start planning, you must have the assurance that you indeed have a tag. Fortunately, most states award tags in the spring when there's plenty of time to prepare for the hunt, but some don't have drawings until summer, making it difficult to plan.

There are three ways of issuing tags. The simplest is the general tag that can be purchased any time prior to the season. There are no quotas, and tags are sold by authorized vendors. As I already mentioned, these general tags are becoming a thing of the past. For example, Colorado was far and away the leader in terms of mule deer hunters. Tags could be purchased across the counter until 1999, when a new law required everyone, including residents, to apply for a tag.

The next way to obtain a tag is to draw it in a lottery. Quotas are established for regions or specific units, and tags are selected via a computer draw. Of course, the more popular the unit, the more competition for tags. Odds are tough in famous units such as a tag in Utah's Paunsagaunt unit or Arizona's Kaibab unit, and drawing one is cause for much celebration. Both produce whopper bucks, and many hunters may apply for years before drawing, if they indeed draw. I drew a Paunsagaunt tag, and considered myself extremely fortunate. I had been applying for a dozen years before I hit pay dirt.

The next way to obtain a tag is to buy it on a first-come, first-served basis. A quota is set, and the tags are sold until they're gone. Idaho is the only state doing this these days (for nonresidents), and the system appears to be working well.

Many states have preference and bonus points that allow the hunter better odds of drawing. The preference point system is a no-fail program that guarantees you a tag provided you accumulate enough points to meet the tag requirement. For example, let's assume you want to hunt a unit that requires five points for a surefire draw. That means you'd have to apply for five years, obtaining one point a year. The number of points required to draw are entirely dependent on the popularity of the unit. A spot that produces megabucks with good public access will obviously require far more points than a neighboring unit with modest bucks and little public access simply because that's where most hunters will want to go.

A bonus point is simply an extra application in the drawing. For example, if you have five bonus points,

you have five applications, and thus five chances of getting a tag. This system is not cumulative; you can draw a tag with zero points or ten points. The odds are in your favor, of course, if you have multiple applications working for you. I had several bonus points when I drew my Utah Paunsagaunt tag, and I attribute my success of drawing the prestigious tag to having those points.

When you plan your hunt, be sure you're keenly aware of point options, and thoroughly go over your application with a fine-tooth comb. Dot every "i" and cross every "t." Your application will be rejected if you make a tiny error. Many states will not inform you of your error, but will send your money back. If a state will indeed inform you, be sure your application is in long before the deadline so you have time to correct and return it.

Be aware that some deadlines are related to the post-mark on your envelope, and others are "in house," which means your application must be at the state

agency office by the deadline. Save yourself the grief of trying to beat the deadline by sending your application in as early as possible.

With the tag confirmed, you must then begin the search for a place to specifically hunt. Your choices will be private, state or federal land. Be aware that much private land in the West is posted, or leased to outfitters or groups of hunters.

On the plus side, tens of millions of acres of federal lands are open to free public hunting in prime mule deer country. The two major agencies are the U.S. Forest Service and the Bureau of Land Management. Generally, Forest Service lands are in the higher elevations, while BLM lands are lower.

Buy maps early on from the agencies whose land you intend to hunt on, and peruse them carefully. Maps are modestly priced, generally less than $5 each. They'll show you land boundaries, road systems and trails, but lack the finer details of topographic maps, which are of much smaller scale. You can order topo maps from the U.S. Geological Survey.

When deciding specifically where to hunt, don't be afraid to call wildlife officers on the phone. If you're polite and not pushy, and ask for general information rather than specific locations, you should be able to obtain valuable advice.

An important decision is your accommodation desires. You can do everything from tent camping to staying in motels. Many hunters haul pickup campers that sit in the bed of a truck, or tow travel campers.

If you're economy minded, you should be able to make a mule deer hunt for less than $1,000, which includes the cost of the nonresident license, travel, food, and accommodations. To make this work, you'll need to drive out with two or three pals who will share the travel cost, camp on public land and plan your meals according to a frugal budget.

Clothing and gear are important considerations. Whether you're hunting in early October or late November, plan on cold weather. See the chapters on clothing and accessories for specifics.

Every western state offers muleys, but, your chances of getting a tag depend enormously on the system of distributing them. For example, Nevada and Arizona offer some of the best mule deer hunting in the West, but tags are extremely tough to obtain. Then too, some western states actually offer far better whitetail hunting than muleys, and in other states there are places where mule deer are of very poor quality. For all these reasons, it's important to inquire long before you plan the hunt so there are no surprises.

TROPHY HOTSPOTS

A trophy mule deer can pop up anywhere, even in places where they're supposed to be absent, or in areas that are whitetail bastions. I've seen some huge muley bucks come from Kansas, Nebraska and North Dakota – states best known for whitetails. But for the serious trophy hunter who wants to hunt a place that consistently produces whopper bucks, I'd suggest a careful analysis of the record book. Generally, here are prime spots in five states that are legendary for their buster bucks.

KEYS

○ = **Top Boone and Crockett Typical Mule Deer Taken Through 1998**   ● = **Top Boone and Crockett Non-Typical Mule Deer Taken Through 1998**   ▨ = **Zumbo's Recommended Trophy Areas**

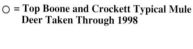

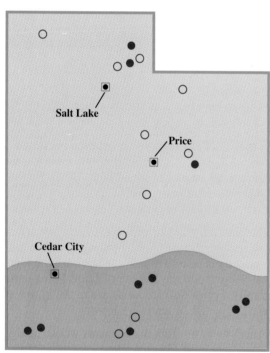

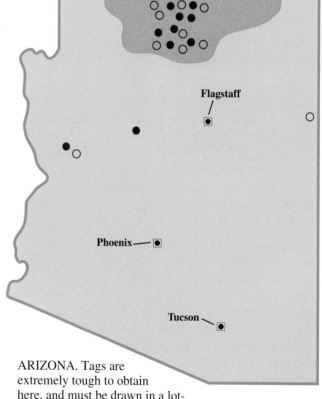

UTAH. Look to the south for megabucks, but you'll need to be lucky to draw a tag. The top unit, and perhaps one of the best in the West, is the Paunsagaunt, which is on the Arizona border. There is good public hunting on the Dixie National Forest and neighboring BLM lands.

ARIZONA. Tags are extremely tough to obtain here, and must be drawn in a lottery. By far the top spot is Coconino County in the north. Big muleys abound here, and there's good public hunting on the Kaibab National Forest.

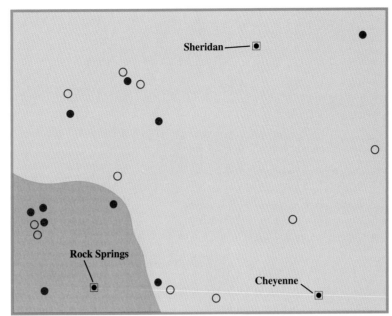

WYOMING. The southwest region is noted for trophy muleys, especially the national forest land on the Bridger-Teton National Forest. The Salt River Range is a top area with good access, but the bigger bucks are taken well away from roads. A tough draw is required for nonresident tags.

Sheridan

Rock Springs

Cheyenne

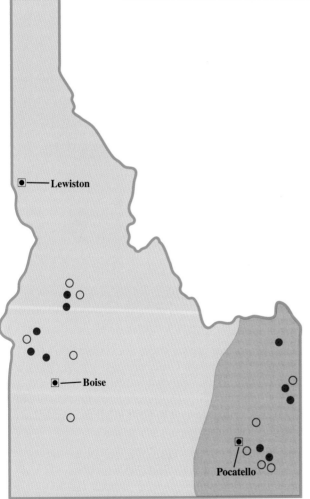

Lewiston

Boise

Pocatello

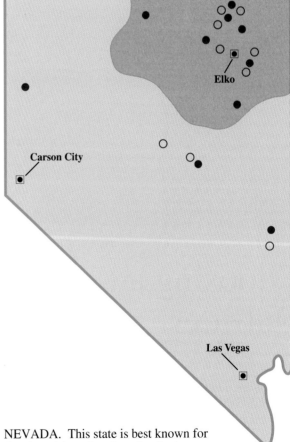

Elko

Carson City

Las Vegas

IDAHO. Nonresident tags are offered on a first-come, first-served basis, and are gone soon after they become available. The prime spot is in the southeast, notably the Caribou National Forest, which borders Wyoming. There's plenty of access here, and the best bucks often come from the backcountry.

NEVADA. This state is best known for dancing girls and casinos, but it gives up very good muleys. Tags must be drawn in a tough lottery. Two spots stand out, Elko County in the northeast and Washoe County in the northwest. There is public hunting available on BLM and U.S. Forest Service lands.

Choosing an Outfitter

There are a number of reasons why hunters hire outfitters to assist them on a mule deer hunt. Many people simply don't know where to go, don't have access, don't know how to hunt mule deer, or don't have gear or the means to transport an animal out of the woods.

Unlike elk, another popular western big-game animal, muleys have far fewer requirements for hunting

them. Mule deer are far more accessible, are often easier to hunt, and certainly are easier to get out of the woods. Having said that, outfitters are a good idea if one is looking for a really good muley or simply wants someone else to tend to all the logistical needs of the hunt.

The first chore to take care of once you've decided to hire an outfitter is to find one who is honest and capable of producing the type of buck you're looking for. Make no mistake, there are plenty of honest outfitters who simply don't have really big bucks. Be sure you communicate with them so they know what you're looking for.

Unfortunately, there are some bad apples in the outfitting business, just as there are shady characters in

where the "guide" would pick you up at dark. Or hunts where one guide was assigned to a half a dozen hunters when the understanding was one guide for two hunters. Or a situation where the hunt lasted only 4 days instead of the 6 days promised, because the other 2 days were "travel" days in and out of camp. And the stories go on and on.

But there are times when outfitted hunts are unsuccessful because the weather hasn't cooperated, or other factors come into play. In some regions, muleys are migratory, and may not move into the hunting area unless enough snow kicks them out of the higher elevations. It's always possible that you might not see a deer if it's a dry, warm fall. This isn't the outfitter's fault, but he'd certainly be at fault if he hadn't told you before you booked about the migratory nature of the deer you're hunting.

A hunt might not work simply because the terrain and vegetation were rugged enough that you couldn't physically get around to where the deer were. Again, that's not the guide's fault, but you should have been told about the rigors of the hunt when you initially discussed it with the outfitter.

WHEN OUTFITTERS ARE A MUST

Outfitters are worth their price in gold, so to speak, in country that's rugged and largely inaccessible to foot travel. One of my favorite mule deer hunting areas is in the Bridger-Teton National Forest in southwest Wyoming. Ridges loom high above the valley floor, and are steep and heavily timbered on the north-facing slopes. Well-worn trails are etched on the tops, carved deeply into the forest floor by untold horses that have walked on them for many decades. It's possible to hunt this country on foot, but it might take most of a day to get to where the big bucks live. A horse can put you there in an hour or two, which is precisely the reason why many hunters opt to hire an outfitter. Some hunters who are savvy to the woods and have basic survival skills will bivouac and pitch a small tent wherever nightfall finds them. I've done that a number of times by myself, but it's a serious game that can have disastrous results if you try it alone and get hurt. The TV show "Survivor" is kindergarten compared to the risks you might take in mountain country. If you opt to hunt solo, be sure you tell someone where you intend to hunt, and give that person a precise time when you expect to return. Be certain to be out of the woods by that agreed-upon time; if you aren't, your contact should immediate call the sheriff or search and rescue.

every other form of business. Many hunters are fleeced by these crooks, because they had no idea what they were in for.

The success of a hunt may be determined by a host of factors. If you don't fill your tag, the outfitter might not be at fault. When I refer to phony outfitters, I'm talking about promises of trophy bucks in places where there are none, poor guides, terrible accommodations, hunting techniques different than those promised, less hunting time than promised, overcrowded camps, and many other negative factors.

I know of instances where a guided hunt meant a trip to the top of the mountain with a so-called guide, then being turned loose with a sandwich and an apple and told to hunt to the bottom of the mountain

Another reason to hire an outfitter is to hunt private lands that are, in all probability, off-limits to the public. You might think that there's no need to hunt private land because of the tens of millions of acres of public acres available to free hunting. That's true, but in reality, much of that public land is woefully crowded with hunters, especially where there's good road access. Then too, many good public areas are in limited-entry units requiring a tough lottery draw, and many are in the backcountry where they're tough to get to. It makes sense to use an outfitter's services to accommodate a hunt on private land.

Years ago, when I worked as a forest ranger, I spent my vacation time guiding for an outfitter in Utah. This was prime mule deer country on his ranch, which was tucked away on a high aspen-covered plateau 30 miles from a highway, and accessible only via four-wheel drive. The deer in that area were big and plentiful. Hunter success was 100 percent, and those hunters were treated to some of the finest mule deer hunting in the country. In one instance, there were so many deer that my hunter simply couldn't make his way through them to stalk close to a buck that he wanted. Too many eyes and ears betrayed us, but eventually we were able to get to a good deer that was within range.

Those kinds of hunts aren't the norm, and it takes some effort to find them. They don't have to be on private land, either, though if they are, you can be sure they're inaccessible to the public or in draw areas. One of my favorite outfitted mule deer hunts was on public land in Wyoming. The outfitter knew his country so well that he almost always knew where to find deer. If he told you to tie your horse up and sneak over to a rim of a ridge and look down, you could expect action at any time.

LISTEN TO THE OUTFITTER

Sometimes hunters second-guess their guides or outfitters and have little confidence in their judgment and decisions.

A buddy of mine, brand-new to mule deer hunting, hunted with a savvy old guide in Montana, and learned a valuable lesson. They were riding horseback through broken country when the guide suddenly spotted a buck 100 yards away. This guide was a man of few words. He seldom spoke, but when he did, you heeded his advice.

"Shoot that buck," the guide said.

My friend got off his horse and looked at the buck through his binoculars.

"How big is he?" the hunter asked.

"Just shoot," replied the guide.

"Will he go 30 inches?" the hunter queried

"Just hurry up and shoot," the guide said, growing impatient with this conversation.

Again my friend hesitated, and the buck whirled and bounded out of sight.

At camp that night, the hunter told me the story, and I chatted with the guide privately afterward.

"How big was that buck?" I asked.

"No idea," the guide responded, "but it was the biggest buck I ever seen in Montana."

On another hunt, this time in Wyoming, I was hunting with an outfitter but had no tag for the unit we hunted that day. My unit was across the valley, but I went along with another hunter just for the ride. The hunter, also a novice to mule deer hunting, rode ahead of me, and at one point the outfitter was around a bend in the trail ahead of us and out of sight.

Suddenly an enormous buck flushed from a patch of brush and ran across a little draw where he stopped and looked at us just below a ridge. I leaped off my horse, grabbed the reins of the hunter's horse, and told him to hurry up and dismount and shoot the buck.

The man got out of the saddle and pulled his rifle out of the scabbard, but he didn't seem to be in a big hurry. In the meantime, I was wild with anxiety, and knew that the monster buck would break and run any moment. The hunter finally raised his rifle and looked at the buck in the scope, but he didn't shoot.

"Hurry and SHOOT," I whispered.

Nothing. The man was making no effort to fire, and the buck still stood there.

"SHOOT, dammit," I said, with a little more volume in my voice.

Then the man said something incredible, and I couldn't believe he said it.

"That's no buck," he said, lowering his rifle, "that's an elk."

I was beside myself, and stammered something to the effect that not only was the animal NOT an elk, but the biggest mule deer buck I'd ever seen.

As expected, the buck took one leap and disappeared over the ridge. The outfitter immediately rode over to us and asked why the hunter hadn't shot. The man didn't know what to say and the very upset outfitter told him that the buck was the biggest he'd ever seen in that area. The hunter, obviously, was not a happy camper, and went home with a much smaller buck.

How to Plan a Mule Deer Hunt

How do you find an ethical outfitter who can offer the type of hunt you're looking for? There are a number of ways, and you should spend plenty of time on this part of the planning stage for your hunt.

THE BOOKING AGENT. The easiest way to locate your outfitter is to let someone else do it for you. A qualified booking agent will carefully consider your needs and locate an outfitter who will meet your terms. The agent should have accumulated a so-called stable of outfitters that he knows well and can trust. In fact, a reputable agent should visit every outfitter's camp he intends to work with to make a first-hand evaluation of the operation. The agent will take care of all the paperwork, and you will probably send him a deposit when you book. The remainder of the cost is normally paid to the outfitter when you arrive for the hunt. Bear in mind that the agent's commission doesn't increase the cost of the hunt. His or her fee is built in, and the commission is paid by the outfitter. In other words, if the hunt cost is normally $2500, you'll pay that price whether you book with an agent or deal directly with the outfitter. Beware that there are shady agents in the business. The idea of making a living by booking hunts and getting free trips to hunting camps is mighty attractive. Unfortunately, many so-called booking agents are so desperate for outfitters that they'll deal with practically anyone, and end up booking for undesirable outfitters. To find a reputable agent, consider one that's been in the business for at least a dozen years, the more the better. These are the established people who know all the ropes and will see that your needs are met in a professional way.

OTHER WAYS. Magazines carry plenty of outfitter ads. Be extra cautious of these, because anyone can buy an ad. When contacting these outfitters, do so by phone, and then ask for brochures. You'll see plenty of pictures of big bucks and smiling hunters in the brochures. Ask how many of these animals were taken in the last couple years. Many brochures will depict bucks that were taken years ago, or worse yet, bucks that weren't taken in the outfitter's area at all. The outfitter will happily provide you with a list of references. Call them, and then ask for the names of other hunters in camp. Call them, too. Of course, only the happy campers will be listed as references. Even in the worst camps, an occasional hunter may get his buck and go home with a smile, even if the rest of the hunters were profoundly dissatisfied.

Sportsmen's shows and hunting conventions are good places to meet outfitters, but again, you must be careful. In fact, some of the worst outfitters are the guys with a big smile and big talk. They'll offer you the moon, but in reality will give you a nightmare hunt. But there are positive reasons to meet potential outfitters in person. It's often possible to size up a person's integrity and honesty by the way he carries himself and communicates. I've found that some of the best outfitters are those who are extremely shy and uncomfortable around strangers, especially urban folks. They aren't bold and outspoken, but find it difficult to communicate.

PHYSICAL EXPECTATIONS. There's an unfortunate notion that an outfitter will offer a hunt that doesn't require much of a physical outlay. That's true in some cases, but many times you'll need to get off the horse or out of the pickup to climb a ridge or hike for a mile or two, maybe more. Be sure to check with the outfitter before you book to learn what might be expected. Ask him about every little detail, and take nothing for granted. Never assume anything, because Murphy's Law is always around the corner.

Do-It-Yourself Mule Deer Hunts

Going on a hunt with just your companions to an unfamiliar place is a challenge, and downright scary if you're going west for the first time. Not only will the land, climate and vegetation be strange, but so will the mule deer.

The first step is to plan precisely where to go, which is covered in a previous chapter in greater detail. With a spot picked and tags obtained, either over the counter or in a lottery draw, you're ready to start preparations. Since you won't have an outfitter to assist in most of your needs, you'll need to plan those details yourself. They include transportation to the hunting area, accommodations once you get there, and how to get the meat from the field to the kitchen. Figure those details out and you've got much of the planning process done.

Most hunters travel to mule deer country in a Suburban, or a pickup with an extended cab. By far,

damage your RV trying to get there. If at all possible, get to the camp area 2 days before the opener (if you're hunting the opener, that is), since most hunters tend to roll in at the last minute.

In much of the West, you should have no problem finding a public campground. Two federal agencies, the U.S. Forest Service and the Bureau of Land Management, together administer about 450 million acres of land in the U.S. (including Alaska). There are national forests in every western state, each of them having campgrounds. On some forests, you must camp only within designed campgrounds during the summer season, but in the fall you can often camp at will. Be sure you know the rules. The BLM has far fewer campgrounds, but on BLM land you can often camp at any spot that strikes your fancy. Most towns have private campgrounds close by, but many are closed after the summer tourist season is over.

It's possible to stay in a motel and hunt mule deer effectively, since many good hunting spots are fairly close to towns. Be aware, however, that many motels are booked well in advance of deer season.

Backpacking into an area away from roads is physically challenging, and only the most hardy hunters will try it. Not only must you haul your gear in on your back, but you must be able to get your deer out as well. Both of these requirements make most hunters think twice before planning a journey of this sort.

In many western towns you can rent horses either by the day, to get your deer out, or for extended periods to move camp in and to use for hunting. Several guest ranches that cater to summer tourists have horses available during hunting season.

It might be to your advantage to stay at one of the many B&B's that are becoming popular everywhere these days. Not only will you have a comfortable place to stay, but you'll have a local contact who might be willing to share information on where you might hunt. Always look for local information, even if it means getting a haircut and chatting with a barber or patronizing a saloon. Be careful in the latter, however, since some folks are wary of strangers who want to hunt "their" country. Nonetheless, you could meet some friendly chaps who would share some information.

If you're keeping an eye on a modest budget, you can easily make a trip for less than $1,000, including the cost of a nonresident license, travel, accommodations, and food. To do this you need to share the cost of driving with two or three other hunters, camp on public land, and keep your food costs down. Doing your own cooking will help with the expenses – better yet, cook meals at home, freeze them, and thaw

most who camp will tow a camp trailer or carry a cab-over camper on a pickup truck. I don't see tents being used as much nowadays as in the past, but hardy hunters still continue to use them. If you intend to camp, you should have a good idea where you're going to set up before you get to the hunt area. This is where map work comes in, but don't rely on it exclusively. The camp you singled out on public land may be closed for the season, or it may be completely full of hunters before you get there. Get on the phone and call the government agency to inquire about the camp, and determine if it's accessible to the type of RV you're towing. Some camps are primitive spots in the backcountry, and you might and heat as required. You can do this with chili, stew, soup, fowl and all sorts of other possibilities. If you're staying in a motel, try to get a room with a kitchenette that will allow you to prepare meals in your room. But keep the menu simple, because you'll be tired when you drag in every night, and won't want to prepare a gourmet feast.

When traveling, designate one person as the banker, and have everyone chip in an equal amount. That money is used for gas, oil, other vehicle expenses and meals, provided everyone chooses a menu that is of average cost. When the money runs out, everyone then adds another equal amount to the bank. That way, you don't have to keep a detailed list of who paid for gasoline the last time, or whatever. Personal items and gifts, of course, are extra and paid for by that individual. The person driving obviously accrues mileage and wear and tear on his vehicle. You can offset that by not requiring him to chip in to the bank, or by designating other drivers on other hunts so everyone has an equal turn.

Getting your venison home isn't necessarily a difficult procedure. This will be covered more thoroughly in the chapter "After the Shot," but basically the bottom line is keeping the meat clean and cool, the latter being far more important. Dirty meat can be trimmed and discarded; warm meat may sour and need to be totally thrown away. Processors are available in practically every small town to cut and package your meat. Carry large coolers with you to bring your meat home.

Other ways to get to your hunt area include taking a bus, train or airplane. I've never known a hunter to travel via train or bus, but plenty of them fly, including me if I don't have the time to drive. Flying presents some special concerns with your firearm and meat. Firearms must be shipped in a hard case, and ammo in separate baggage and in its original box. Meat is best shipped in coolers, which can't exceed 70 pounds; those that do will be shipped air freight and you'll be charged a considerable sum. If you use dry ice, you MUST inform the airline clerk when you check in. Most airlines allow you to check two bags; anything over that will be charged extra.

One of the biggest fears in hunting a new spot is precisely where to hunt. Rest assured that you won't have much of a problem finding public land in most parts of mule deer country. When I first headed west in 1960 to study forestry in Utah, I'd never been any farther west than Pennsylvania. Imagine my surprise when I gazed upon millions upon millions of acres of federal land that had no posted signs. One could walk for days and never trespass on private land. That's still the case today – those lands are still very

much intact, but what's different is a modern attitude among many landowners. Don't be surprised to learn that ranches in prime mule deer country are posted, many of them leased to outfitters or groups of hunters. There are no exceptions in most states – virtually every acre is locked up. Ranchers have learned that wildlife has a value, and that they can often make more money from hunters than they can from crops or domestic livestock. I surely don't condemn ranchers for trying to make a living, but it's a sad commentary on what's happening in the field – in every part of the country.

You'll note that much of the land in the valley bottoms and foothills is privately owned, and much federal land – especially BLM – is entirely inaccessible, blocked by private land. To understand this, you need to look back to the days when the West was homesteaded. Pioneers quickly staked their claims in the bottoms, where there was water and fertile land for ranching and agriculture. That being the case, you might be frustrated at being unable to gain access to those public lands. Elsewhere in this book I've offered a solution to getting on much of that land, if you're willing to work at it.

If you're willing to spend a bit more money, you can hire an outfitter to take you to a drop camp. On the plus side, you'll be transported, usually on horseback, to an established camp and dropped off to hunt on your own. The outfitter will return for you at a predetermined time and pack you and your deer out. Camp basically consists of a sleeping tent and cooking tent, or perhaps a very large tent that serves both purposes. There is usually a supply of firewood, and basic camp gear, such as lanterns, cookstove, woodstove, cots, utensils and other items. Don't make any assumptions or trust that everything will be provided. Double-check with the outfitter so there are no misunderstandings. Ideally, your drop camp will be situated in a prime area where you'll have exclusive hunting opportunities at big bucks, with no competition from other hunters. But don't count on it. There's a big downside to many drop camps. Because of the relatively small profit, some outfitters aren't willing to establish them in prime spots where extra effort is required to set them up. Then too, outfitters typically place their higher-paying clients in the best camps, keeping the drop camp hunters well away so there's no competition. Outfitters are also aware that people who go to drop camps are more prone to accept hardships, and therefore might return on their own in later years, thus offering competition to the outfitter.

Check drop camps carefully before you book. They could be the site of the best hunts of your life or the very worst.

Drop Camps

It sounds too good to be true. An outfitter takes you and your pals on horseback to an established camp in prime deer country. When you dismount, you look over the camp, complete with a sleeping tent, cook tent, utensils, lanterns, cots, a stack of firewood and everything else you would want in the backcountry. And best of all, you're plunked down in a superb place to hunt mule deer, and can hunt at your leisure with your pals. You won't have to follow a guide, or meet a predetermined schedule. You're on your own, and the price is right – a whole lot less than if you'd booked a guided hunt. What more can you ask? The outfitter takes away the guesswork in locating deer country, provides you with a camp, and transports your game back to the trailhead at the end of the hunt.

There are some downsides, however, just as there are negatives with many "too good to be true" adventures. A minor disadvantage is the need to do all the camp chores, including cooking, washing dishes, splitting firewood and other tasks. A major negative, however, is the possibility of being set up in a place that has few, if any, of the deer you're hoping to find. Some unscrupulous outfitters will establish drop camps in marginal country because it isn't cost effective to go the extra mile, so to speak, and set up a camp in a more distant area.

Outfitters may also be reluctant to set up drop camps close to their fully guided areas because of the competition from drop camp hunters. Then too, people who go to drop camps are often more independent and hardy than those who must be guided, and outfitters don't want more competition in later years from former drop camp hunters who may go back to that area on their own.

The best way to check out a drop camp is to ask the outfitter the general area where he'll be taking you and then do some research with the wildlife agency. Don't ask the outfitter to pinpoint the camp, because most won't. Obviously he won't want to disclose the whereabouts of his hunting areas to strangers.

Before heading to camp, be certain you check out the details with the outfitter. Even the most insignificant items could be a serious problem, such as inoperative lantern mantles, an insufficient supply of stove fuel, a broken axe handle, missing cooking utensils, no toilet paper, and many other seemingly minor items. Make sure you know precisely how your game will be transported from camp. You might have to get your deer to the camp area by a predetermined date. In some cases, the outfitter will check on you every couple days and take your game out. What you don't want in a drop camp is surprises. Do your homework, and make sure the only surprises are positive ones.

Scouting

The most consistently successful hunters I know are familiar with the areas they hunt. They understand the habits of the quarry, and where the animals eat, sleep and hide. When you come down to it, whether you're hunting quail, rabbits, mule deer or moose, it's a big advantage to know everything you can about the animal or bird you're hunting and the area it lives in.

If you don't live in the West and have never been to the area you intend to hunt, you should make every effort to arrive a few days prior to your hunt to do some intense scouting. If you don't have the luxury of those few days, at least one day is recommended, giving you a few hours to take a cursory look; then you can learn more while you actually hunt.

Scouting should first begin on paper. You should do your homework with updated maps and a telephone. (See the chapter, "Do-It-Yourself Deer Hunts.") Once you've established the general area where you're going to hunt, you'll need to determine where and how you'll overnight, and specifically where you intend to hunt. That's best done firsthand, by visiting the place and looking it over.

Scouting is often considered an activity where you hike around your unit before the season and look for deer sign. It's that, of course, but much more. The most important thing to do on your initial visit is to determine the legal boundaries of the area you're hunting. Be sure you know precisely, and not generally, the area you can hunt. Know exactly which fence or ridgeline marks the boundary, and mark those locations with a GPS if you have one or on the most updated map you can acquire.

Once you know the boundaries, roll up your sleeves and go to work. The next step is to try to locate escape cover, feeding areas, bedding areas and major trails that connect everything together. Escape cover may be the most critical part of your search if you're hunting public land and there's plenty of pressure. That being the case, muleys may abandon their normal routine and shift their behavior to include the densest cover they can find. Of course, you should seek prominent feeding areas, as well as identifying trails that lead to bedding cover. Be aware that deer might not bed in heavy vegetation, but in and around shrubs, or even in sagebrush that isn't much more than 2 feet high. Your efforts should be directed according to the habitat in which you're hunting.

It's always smart to find water sources, especially in arid places such as the high desert or in sagebrush or pinyon juniper country where water sources are scarce and located a long distance apart. Look for these places by talking with people intimate with the land. If you're hunting BLM or Forest Service land, go to the administrative office and ask to see land surface maps that show waterholes. These are usually identified, since livestock distribution is governed by the availability of water, and government land is normally divided into grazing units. Each unit typically holds a certain number of range cows or sheep, and these animals are allowed in the unit only during specific times. It's a wise idea to determine when livestock will use the place you intend to hunt. If 3,000 sheep graze in your hunting area during your hunt, deer may temporarily leave, since muleys often don't socialize with sheep. In some cases they aren't fond of cattle either. This may be because of the noise generated by domestic animals. Perhaps deer are insecure because they can't hear very well.

TALK TO THE LOCALS

Sheepherders and cowboys are superb sources of information. They'll not only be able to tell you where the water is, but where they've seen big bucks. Many of these folks are willing to share information, since very few of them hunt and most aren't trying to guard secret spots. Other workers such as people working oil and gas fields may have a wealth of information, along with forest rangers, range technicians, forest surveyors, and other folks who are familiar with the country you hunt. Sometimes it's wise to reward valuable sources of information with little gifts from your homeland. For example, I know hunters from California who bring plenty of fresh citrus to give away, Washington hunters who bring apples and New England hunters who carry small tins of maple syrup. If your region isn't noted for anything, homemade cookies always work. Be careful about handing out alcohol. This could cause a problem that you didn't anticipate.

Scouting is almost mandatory if you're a serious trophy hunter. Some hunters literally want to locate specific bucks if they can, and try to pattern their movements. This would be far easier on lowland environments such as ranch, agriculture and desert lands because deer are more visible and their movement patterns aren't as large and difficult to trace as they are in forested mountain country. If you spot deer early in the morning and they aren't disturbed by you or other hunters, chances are good they'll remain there over the course of several days. Try to locate as many herds as possible by staying on ridges and doing a lot of glassing. Muleys are easiest to see when the sun first appears in the morning. The rays seem to shine off their coats and also easily betray their light-colored rumps.

It's extremely important to remember that the deer you spot before the season opens may be long gone before opening morning. Muleys know that the sudden influx of people and the attendant noises and smells mean danger. Wary bucks will disappear quickly, never to be seen again. That's why it's so very important to find escape cover where deer will hide out.

It may be a waste of time to scout on public land near good access if there are plenty of people around. Any deer easily spotted will be pursued by many hunters. It's best to find an out-of-the-way place where you can locate undisturbed animals. That might not be easy to do in places that receive high hunting pressure.

Sign that shows the presence of animals includes evidence of feeding, such as freshly nipped twigs on preferred browse species like bitterbrush and mountain mahogany. The presence of droppings might not be helpful unless you can determine how fresh they are. Droppings may remain on the ground for months or even years, depending on the climate. Don't count on an abundance of shed antlers as being an indicator of mule deer activity, since antlers are shed in the winter months, and deer may not be in those areas during the fall hunting season. They might be miles away.

Scouting is an extremely important component of mule deer hunting. Whenever you can, learn the country and the deer habits before the season opens. It's no fun to find that special spot on the afternoon of the last day you can hunt. That's happened to me more times than I can remember, and always when I didn't have time to scout thoroughly.

Locked Out of Public Land? Try This.

Much of the best mule deer country in the West is private land, and practically all of it is posted, especially if it offers prime hunting. Outfitters lease much of it, as do hunting groups. Unfortunately, many private lands butt up to public lands, and access onto the public lands seems to be blocked. But don't despair. Many of those chunks of land are accessible on one or more sides. With some astute mapwork and legwork, you might be able to hunt them. And because those public lands require some effort to get to, they're often largely unhunted.

First, get an updated map that clearly shows boundaries, and make sure the public land you're interested in has an approachable route. In order for this method to work, you must make your original access off a county or public road directly on public land, and carefully work your way to the spot you want to hunt. This might involve a mile or more of hiking, crossing creeks, climbing rockslides, etc., but the effort is often worth it. Many hunters shun those public lands, believing they're blocked by the private property. It's worth repeating: be sure of your route and that you stay on public land all the way. A GPS unit will help eliminate guesswork.

Physical Conditioning

Since mule deer live in so many different environments, from deserts to the alpine tundra, the physical challenge in hunting them depends largely on the nature of their habitat. If you tackle them in the mountains, for example, where much mule deer hunting occurs, then you'll need to be in far better shape than if you hunt them in agricultural areas. It's a safe statement that little mule deer country in the prime states is flat. There's almost always a need to hike up slopes or descend them, putting strain on an unexercised urban body.

You can, of course, drive around all day in your pickup or roar around the hills in your ATV. That's your choice. But even so, you might spot the buck of your dreams staring at you from a high ridge where your fancy vehicle won't take you (or where it's illegal to take it off road), and you'll find yourself huffing and puffing up a steep slope that you never intended to climb.

My suggestion, unless you're lucky enough to have drawn a mule deer tag in Kansas, or another likewise flat spot, is to be prepared for the worst. The most consistently successful hunters I know head for the hills and mountains afoot with a loaded daypack and plenty of enthusiasm and determination. But back to Kansas. Don't be fooled into thinking that this is an easy proposition, either. Walking rapidly for several miles even on relatively flat ground isn't necessarily a piece of cake. And if you've ever walked a mile across a plowed field, you may still remember the pain. Doubly so if it was a muddy field. The bottom line: don't count on any mule deer hunt to be easy unless you intend to sit in a treestand and stay there.

A complete physical is a wise idea before you head out on your trip, especially if you're 40 years old or more. You might need to lose some weight and begin an exercise program to get in shape. If you're hunting in high elevations, which is the case in most mule deer country, your body will react by working harder. Your legs, lungs and heart will have a tougher time adjusting to the sudden strain of moving about in steep terrain, and the reduced oxygen will have an effect as well. If you hunt in the Rockies, you can figure that most of your hunting will be at the 6,000- to 9,000-foot level.

Back problems are major ailments, and there isn't much you can do to help other than to avoid twisting your body, or bending and lifting things incorrectly. I wear a back brace any time I'm involved in any unusual strain, even when hiking about in the mountains. If your back goes out, your mule deer hunt will come to an abrupt halt. You might bring along some muscle relaxants or other medication, but rely on your doctor's advice.

Acute mountain sickness (AMS) can strike without warning and affects about 30 percent of us. It isn't caused by too much exercise, but by the mere fact of being in the higher elevations. Symptoms may include dizziness, lightheadedness, headache, nausea and fatigue. The remedy, in most cases, is simply to descend to lower elevations.

The act of getting a deer out can be a major ordeal, and can cause serious physical injury because of the exertion required. Always pace yourself with the task at hand, and don't take on any more than you think you can. A hernia, back injury or worse can be the result.

Remember that mule deer live in big country, and you might be required to work far harder than you thought. Prepare to work hard and use your good judgment. No deer is worth a serious injury or ailment.

Hunting Techniques

Glass & Stalk

Because much mule deer country is fairly open, stalking is an excellent option. By stalking, I mean first spotting a deer that is out of range with the naked eye, binoculars or spotting scope, and then moving to an acceptable shooting position. This can be done by either sneaking up to the deer unseen, or positioning yourself so the animal walks into an ambush.

Since stalking depends on seeing a deer and remaining undetected, it's best to begin your search early in the morning, glassing for deer before legal shooting light. Muleys will feed in the daylight if hunter pressure is minimal, giving you the opportunity to move in for a shot. If undisturbed, deer may bed as late as 2 hours or more after sunrise, but that depends on the particular deer you're hunting. A wary old buck may be bedded before shooting hours, even if there's very little hunter activity. More than once I've seen a big buck lie down before sunrise.

Ideally, watching a buck bed down from a distance is the best of all worlds. You'll have the rest of the day to work the wind and the terrain, and catch him napping. But it may not be as easy as it sounds. If you're able to see the animal bed down, he's probably in fairly open country, making it difficult to put on a sneak without being spotted. Of course, he might have bedded in a pocket of brush – you know he's in there, but you don't know exactly where he's bedded. Some time ago I was glassing a distant sidehill and saw a bedded buck looking squarely at me and my companion. He was at least a half mile away and it took some time to make a big circle and come up behind him. We were making a final approach when I realized he wasn't where I'd seen him. He'd relocated 30 yards away, and he caught us off guard by bouncing through the rocks and making a clean escape. On another hunt my companion and I watched a distant buck standing on a ridge. He stood motionless for more than 10 minutes and finally walked into a big pile of huge boulders and brush. I waited for a half hour, and could see every exit possibility. Since the cover was barely 10 yards wide and surrounded by sagebrush, I was fairly certain he'd bedded within. We made a circle and very carefully eased up from the ridge behind the boulders. It was snowing softly and the stalk was as perfectly silent as any I'd ever made. At one point I was standing on a rock and peered below me. Not 3 yards away I saw the nose and muzzle of the buck. He was chewing his cud, peacefully looking out into the sagebrush. I turned to tell my companion about the buck and my clothing barely touched a twig. The deer immediately catapulted out of his bed and instantly vanished around the bend. Both those stalks were right out of the textbook, but we were foiled at the last minute. Any time you move close to a bedded deer, you're going to be tested mightily by his superb ears.

PLANNING THE STALK

Before beginning any stalk, form a mental picture in your mind of the position of the deer and the various options for making the approach. Carefully analyze every possible route, noting terrain features and available screening cover. Be absolutely certain that the wind is favorable when you decide on the approach.

The next step is extremely important, and one that's overlooked by many hunters. Before leaving your vantage point, make mental notes of the deer's precise position by referencing the deer to landmarks. Be sure that you can identify those landmarks from the angle that you'll be making your approach, realizing that everything looks different when viewed from a different angle.

Sometimes it's absolutely impossible to get close to a deer that you know is bedded because the terrain is completely open and there's no way to approach within decent shooting range. You'll have two options if alone, and another if you have a companion. If hunting solo, you can get as close as possible, use a comfortable and steady rest, and make a long shot, but only if you're

confident that you can make it. The other option is to find a spot where you can wait the buck out until he finally gets to his feet in late afternoon to begin his feeding routine. In that case, you're hoping he'll move closer to you as he feeds along. If you have a partner, you might send him or her to a designated spot where an unseen approach can be made, and then drive the deer in the direction you want. That's always iffy, and has about a 50-50 chance of succeeding unless you can position your companion near an obvious escape area, such as a deep canyon or patch of heavy timber. In that case, chances are good the spooked buck will head in that direction.

Trying to set up an ambush is a workable technique if the vegetation is open enough to give you a good view. If possible, I'll move rapidly, using the terrain to my advantage, to a high spot overlooking the route I think the deer will be using. I'll want to be at that spot long before the animals arrive, so I can then make another move quickly if they change direction. The idea here is to make some educated guesses as to where the deer are headed so you can cut them off at the pass, so to speak.

When making any kind of approach, be aware that muleys have superb vision. Do everything you can to stay out of sight, even if it means crawling commando-style with your rifle cradled in your arms. Beware of cactus, by the way, since it grows practically everywhere in mule deer country.

Using Landmarks

My daughter Judi and I stalked her first buck in open sagebrush country after spotting the deer at first light. The buck was with three does, and we watched the deer disappear over a rise with the exception of one doe that bedded just under the opposite side of the rise. I could see just her ears and the top of her head through a spotting scope and assumed that the rest of the deer were lying close by but out of sight. I knew we were in for a complicated stalk because of the open country, and before heading out I noted a trio of old fenceposts on top of the ridge close to the deer. There were no other landmarks. To make the stalk, Judi and I made a large circle that took well more than an hour, and I noted that the fenceposts were out of view. I also realized that there was a series of similar ridges running about, and it was virtually impossible to tell where the deer were from our position as we traveled. Finally I saw one of the posts, and we maneuvered until the other two came into view. Only then did I know exactly where the deer were. A half hour later we made the final approach and caught the buck unaware. Judi had her first buck tagged a moment later.

Early-Season Muleys

The term "early season" usually refers to the period prior to the general firearms season that opens in mid-October to early November in most states. Bowhunters are usually afield in September, and in some cases, in August. Rifle hunters who hunt early either draw special limited-entry tags or opt to hunt in backcountry units where seasons are held in September.

In mountain country, mule deer are typically in the upper elevations until snow forces them to winter range. September hunting often means plenty of climbing and hiking, often in very hot weather. Deer are scattered over an enormous area, though big bucks often group together in bachelor herds. Finding those bucks may take some doing, because they often don't move much in warm weather. They'll typically bed high, often in and around rimrock ridges if they exist, or at the edge of timberline. They'll often bed very early, sometimes at sunrise, making them even more difficult to locate. Trying to hunt these high-country bucks on foot is a major effort, because you often must begin hiking in the dark to reach them by shooting light.

In one of my favorite early-season spots, I camp in a valley next to a stream along a forest service road, and begin climbing long before the first traces of gray in the eastern sky. I'll walk a well-used horse trail to start my journey, but after hiking on it an hour or so, putting me a couple miles from the road, I'll turn off and walk out on a ridge where there are no horse trails. Outfitters normally ride the trails with their clients, but seldom venture very far away from their horses. To deer living in the high country, just one party of hunters on a trail each day is enough to force them into hiding, and they'll seek cover in small basins and pockets well away from those trails. I'll stay in the high country until the last minute of shooting light, and use my flashlight to find my way back down after dark. Since I'm so far from my truck, I'll leave room in my pack to carry boned meat, and I'll also bring plenty of rope so I can lash a quarter of meat on and carry it out if I decide to bone it rather than quarter it. That decision depends on the distance I have to transport the meat, and the air temperature. By boning it I can carry more meat and cool it more quickly by hanging it in meat bags in the shade as I work. The mountain breezes will usually take the heat away fairly rapidly.

Some or all of the bucks you'll see in early September may still be wearing velvet on their antlers. If that's the case, the deer will appear to be much larger than they are because of the velvet covering. Look the buck over carefully before taking the shot if you're trophy hunting and want an outsized buck. Since bucks may hang out in small groups, don't be too hasty in making a decision to shoot if you see only one or two animals. Bigger bucks may be lying nearby, hidden from view by brush or the lay of the land. Try to ease about for a better look, giving yourself the opportunity to spot additional deer. More than once a hunter learned that he shot the smallest buck of the bunch because he was too impatient to look for more deer.

Because deer haven't been hammered by crowds yet, early-season bucks might not take off in an explosive flush and run out of the country as they might during the regular season. However, a big buck that's learned to survive many seasons will usually be elusive and wary. Don't assume he'll be an easy quarry.

If you can, hike to the highest point you can find before shooting light and use your binoculars extensively. Start your search close in, and than increase the distance. If you spot a good buck a long way off, watch him to see where he goes, or if he beds down. In the latter case, plan the rest of the day accordingly, making your approach with the wind in your favor. If it's a quiet, dry day, consider the noise factor as well. It might be better to make a longer but quieter approach on sandstone or rimrock, for example, than a shorter approach through brush and leaves. If the deer are a long way off and the terrain and vegetation are such that you don't want to try sneaking on them in their beds, consider leaving them alone for the day, but returning to set up an ambush in late afternoon. If undisturbed, muleys will often return to the same places they fed in the morning. Again, be observant of that all-important wind.

Because early-season deer are hunted during warm weather, always be concerned with care of the meat. It must be protected from heat, flies, birds and four-legged critters if you leave it overnight. It often takes more effort to hunt deer early, but the lack of hunters in backcountry allows more solitude as well as the opportunity to see some trophy bucks. This is a time for serious hunters who aren't afraid to get away from roads and expend some physical effort. You might very well see some of the biggest bucks of your life, and all in one group. That's a common reward and plenty of motivation for some hunters to hunt early.

Stand Hunting

Whereas treestands are popular among whitetail hunters, you'll see few of them used by mule deer hunters, primarily because the home range of a muley is much larger than that of a whitetail, and mule deer are more vagabond in nature, covering far more country during their daily movements. There are some exceptions in lower elevations, especially on ranches and farms, where mule deer have more firmly established routes between feeding and bedding areas.

By and large, most stand hunting is done from the ground, where there is good visibility over a wide area. Whenever possible, I'll select a site on top of a ridge, where I can see an opposing slope. Better yet, I'll find a vantage point that offers a view as close to 360 degrees as possible. I'll be equipped with good binoculars and a spotting scope, and I'll be in the stand long before the first light.

If there are other hunters in the woods, I'll find a spot that muleys will use as an escape route between feeding and security areas. For example, I hunted in Colorado amidst a small army of hunters. It was mountainous country, with oak brush and aspens growing in thick patches. A deep canyon ran adjacent to the cover, and I was reasonably sure that it was being used as a refuge by spooked deer. I positioned myself near a well-used trail that led down into the canyon, arriving there in the dark. The shooting started soon after legal shooting hours, and I saw two dozen hunters moving about in the cover.

Presently a small herd of deer bounded toward me, headed directly for the canyon. One was a modest buck, sporting antlers that were about 20 inches wide, and I was considering taking him when a much larger buck appeared. He wasn't moving as quickly as the others, but was more cautious, stopping and looking every now and then. He was just about to drop into the canyon and had taken one last look when I settled the crosshairs behind his shoulder. He was a dandy, a large-bodied animal with a 27-inch-wide rack.

When you select a vantage point, be sure you can be mobile if the need arises in order to get to deer that are too far for a shot. Be positive, too, that you can physically get to the area. I met a hunter once who was watching a slope directly across from him, about 300 yards away. There were deer moving on it, but there was a major problem. A deep, uncrossable river was at the bottom of the ridge, preventing him

from getting to a deer if he shot one. In many areas, vertical cliffs can also become impossible obstacles.

Be sure that once you leave your observation post you can find the spot you're headed to. The view will change as you move, and you might not be able to locate the spot you want to reach. Look for landmarks and use them to keep your bearings. Sometimes a compass won't help you either, because you might have to skirt large areas that can't be negotiated.

When I first get to the stand area, I'll settle in and make myself comfortable. Then I'll use my binoculars as the morning light gradually improves. When it's light enough to see a long way off, I'll scan the countryside without the binoculars, looking for the telltale white rump that often betrays muleys, especially when the sun is low in the sky. Then I'll use the binoculars to check out deer I've spotted, and if I haven't located any I'll bring the binoculars into play again, looking into shaded spots, along the edge of cover, and into patches of brush where deer may be feeding. In the case of long-range deer, I'll check them out with my spotting scope.

STAYING PATIENT

I'll stay at my vantage point longer than usual if there are other hunters about, since they might drive deer to me. Typically I'll vacate a stand site around midmorning and then try another strategy, unless plenty of deer are in the area and hunters are continually moving them around. There's an old saying that some of the best hunting is between 10 a.m. and 2 p.m. I believe one of the reasons this is so is that hunters become restless and perhaps uncomfortable in cold weather, and head for camp, pushing yet more deer around.

In lower elevations, I'll be on a stand in the dark where I can look into feeding areas, such as sagebrush flats, and then, if necessary, move into cover where deer are heading to bedding spots. Once the sun is firmly above the eastern horizon, I'll spend more time looking into thicker areas than openings, though deer may walk through them to get to bedding areas if unpressured by other hunters.

Scouting before the opener is always a good idea in order to determine stand positions. If you don't have

the time to scout early, then take a hike after you've made a morning hunt and look over as much country as possible. Try to determine where other hunters are coming from, and check for fresh sign of feeding deer. Though muleys aren't as easily patterned as whitetails, they indeed use trails, and it's always a good idea to watch active trails when deer movement occurs early in the morning and late in the afternoon.

Always consider the wind when evaluating your stand location. It's not usually critical if you're on a ridge and the wind is at your back, but remember that in the West, the thermal breezes normally blow down the slope in the night and up the slope in the day.

Don't be afraid to walk a little farther to your stand, even if you can drive to it in your pickup or ATV. The noise made by your vehicle may spook deer. Besides, competition between hunters being what it is, you might want to park your rig some distance away to decoy hunters to another spot. That might not sound very nice, but it's a reality of hunting. Competition between hunters is a very important aspect of the sport.

Driving

There's an interesting notion about driving deer. Some hunters believe that well-executed drives will put the deer exactly where you want them. That, unfortunately, is a false assumption, since deer will go where THEY want to go, and not where the drivers want them to go.

A deer drive, also called a "push," is basically a strategy where two groups of hunters team up to move deer from cover, and into an ambush situation. One part of the team, called the drivers or pushers, attempts to rout deer into the waiting arms of the standers. Sometimes this strategy is enormously successful; other times it's a dismal failure. One of the biggest reasons it fails is simply because no deer are present in the area being driven. Another reason is because muleys fail to cooperate according to the game plan and either refuse to be routed, or exit from an unexpected route.

PLANNING A DRIVE

There are two types of drives, the noisy drive and the quiet drive. Each has its followers who believe their technique is best. The noisy drive involves walking through cover, banging a stick on trees, talking, shouting, blowing whistles and basically making as much noise as possible. The idea is to spook deer and get them on their feet, encouraging them to run wildly off toward a waiting stander. The quiet drive is done by slowly slipping through the woods, stopping often and making as little human sound as possible. Proponents of the quiet drive claim that muleys are more unnerved by silent humans moving through cover, and are more apt to rush off, since the deer can't pinpoint the danger. In the noisy drive, deer can easily track the location of hunters and take evasive action.

For safety reasons, the noisy drive is best, since standers can determine exactly where the drivers are. In a quiet drive, the drivers are, of course, much more difficult to keep track of.

Before planning a drive, many variables must be considered, such as the type of cover, steepness of the terrain, probable escape routes, the number of drivers and standers, and wind direction. In general, flushed deer typically run uphill initially. Once they've made it to a ridgetop they might head for higher ground, or run to a thicket or timber stand that offers security cover.

The major reasons that drives fail include the carelessness of standers moving toward their positions, human noise they make when on stand, and the failure to consider wind direction. There's a perception that deer being driven will run smack into a stander because of the animal's haste to get away. That's not always so. A deer running from hunters is at full alert, and quite often in tune with danger ahead of him as well as behind him. If a stander is spotted, heard or smelled, rest assured that the deer will quickly change directions and try another escape route. It's imperative that the drive be designed so the standers won't be betrayed by the wind. The standers must also take a position where they're screened by cover so they won't be easily seen by deer. It's also necessary to sneak quietly into the stand location, and to be absolutely silent; deer are likely to make a detour around that spot if they hear a person there.

When determining where to place the standers, it's always tempting to position them at the end of the drive. After all, it's logical that spooked deer will run straight away from danger and exit cover at the far end. But don't count on it. Again, deer can't be driven where we want them to go. That being the case, it's necessary to figure likely escape routes to place the standers. Muleys have a bad rap for being dumb, and that's an unfortunate assumption. Rather than busting out of cover and running boldly in the open, many deer, especially educated bucks, will use escape routes that offer screening cover, such as fingers of timber that connect one patch of trees to another. Many deer will escape the drive area by bounding out through the flanks, and some deer may run between the drivers and break out of the cover where the drive began. It's always a good idea, if you have enough standers, to place one where the drivers initially entered the woods.

Before starting the drive, a safety briefing is in order, if nothing other than a reminder that many people are concentrated in a small area, and extreme care is the priority of the day. Everyone should wear hunter orange, even if it isn't required by law. The use of two-way radios to alert or direct hunters to game is unethical, immoral and in many states, illegal. I believe the deer deserves better.

Tracking

It seems simple – all you do is locate a set of fresh tracks, follow them, and shoot your buck. Nice thought, but seldom realistic. The tracking strategy might be one of the toughest of all, because the quarry has an uncanny way of quickly discerning danger behind it.

Snow is, of course, the primary medium to track in. Very few hunters have the skill to follow a deer in dirt or sand, and there are few habitats that offer the conditions whereby you can do so. An exception is Sonora, in Mexico, where guides track huge muleys for miles in the sand. It's not uncommon for a guide to locate a fresh track in the morning, and stay with it until dark, resuming the next day.

A major dilemma in tracking is determining the freshness of the track. Obviously, you don't want to follow a deer if it passed by 3 days ago. The easiest way is to literally see the deer walking in the distance, and then immediately pick up its track in the snow. There's no question how old it is. If you're lucky enough to be in that situation, don't rush off immediately to start tracking. Pick a landmark close to where you spotted the deer, and go to that location. This insures that you won't be following the trail of another buck that walked by earlier unbeknown to you. It's possible that there could be a maze of tracks concentrated in a small area.

The next best thing to seeing the deer is to track during or immediately after a snowfall. In that case there's no question that the track is fresh. And if you're following the track during a storm and the prints have no snow in them, then carry your rifle in the ready position and be prepared for an imminent shot.

But what about the tracking conditions when snow has been on the ground for days? It can be mighty tough to figure out the age of the tracks. Generally, look at the edges of the tracks and see how crisp they are, how much they've thawed, and if there's crumbled snow or forest debris in them. These are all clues that can help you determine their age. Consider the air temperature patterns of the last day or two to figure when the tracks might have thawed or refrozen.

Can you tell if the deer you're following is a buck or doe? I've heard all sorts of "foolproof" techniques, but I claim it's impossible. Some people say that bucks leave dewclaw prints and that does do not. Others say that the stride of the animal or the way it urinates are other clues. Again, I'm not convinced. The only way to really tell is to see the deer standing in the tracks. About the only clue I'll accept is the size of the track. Bucks are generally considerably heavier than does, which means their tracks will be larger in size, and probably deeper in the snow because of the weight factor.

The pattern of the tracks can often give you a clue as to where the deer is headed or what it's doing. If the tracks meander about in and out of brush, you can often figure the animal is feeding. This is reinforced if you see evidence that the deer has been pawing in the snow to get at forbs and grasses. In the event that the tracks are lined out, the deer is probably headed directly to a feeding or bedding area, especially if it's on a trail.

TRACKING TIPS

Let's say you're following a smoking set of fresh tracks. What precautions should you consider? First, assume that the deer is always looking back at you. It won't be, of course, unless you're detected, but you should be of the mindset that the animal ahead of you is totally alert to danger. Knowing this, you don't hike along boldly, hoping to spot the animal and shoot it handily. Instead, you slip and ease forward, always expecting to see the quarry, perhaps bedded. Use your binoculars whenever possible.

If you're in mountainous terrain, take advantage of a slope, if you can, by climbing high above the trail to where you can see ahead. You might be able to see the deer ahead of you from that elevated position. Of course, you must be able to key in on the track to know that you haven't strayed away from it.

Be sure you wear clothing that is silent, and refrain from making any unnecessary noise. The quarry will be tuned to the sights, sounds and smells around it.

What happens if you jump the deer and don't get a shot? Be prepared for that eventuality, because it will happen far more than not. The best recourse is to stay put and be quiet for at least 15 minutes. Then, very quietly, and with more caution than ever, pick up the track, but be aware that the animal that you're now following is nervous and aware of your presence. You'll have a tough job seeing it before it sees you. That challenge is one of the toughest of all.

Tracking excites me if I know the quarry is not far away. It's a one-on-one proposition, just me and the deer. If I fail, it's my fault because there's no guesswork. The deer is very much there; it's my job to find him. Can it get any better than that?

Stillhunting

Mule deer are immensely fun to hunt by stillhunting. It's my favorite hunting strategy, because it offers the challenge of moving quietly through cover and spotting a deer before it sees you. That's the essence of stillhunting, which, properly defined, means slipping through the vegetation at a snail's pace. It doesn't mean being still; in this sense it's a confusing term to newcomers to hunting.

Whether you stillhunt in aspens, or evergreen forests, or pinyon-juniper forests, or wherever, the technique is basically the same. You do everything possible to gain the advantage of being undetected by the quarry. This means working with the current weather conditions, wearing the appropriate clothing and using the best gear for the situation at hand. Let's examine each of these in detail.

WEATHER. The wind is of paramount importance, and must be considered when you stillhunt, even if it means that you must go some distance out of the way to work into the wind. Remember that muleys have superb noses, and if they detect your scent, they'll be long gone before you show up. I prefer stillhunting on windy days because the sound of the wind through the vegetation covers the noise I make while walking. There are disadvantages, however, especially if the wind isn't from a prevailing direction, but is variable. On many occasions I've had the frustrating experience of seeing the wind blow from practically every direction over the course of 15 minutes. When that happens, all you can do is to continue and hope for the best, trying to figure if the wind is from a fairly constant direction and working with it as best you can.

Rain is often welcome when you stillhunt, as long as it doesn't pour buckets, distracting you and making you so uncomfortable you can't hunt effectively. My idea of perfect stillhunting weather is a slight prevailing breeze and a steady light rain. It's obvious that if the ground is wet, you'll be able to walk quietly, and the sound of rain hitting the vegetation often helps cover up the noise you make.

Snow may or may not be an asset when you stillhunt. It will help to make deer more obvious in the white background, but it will also make you more visible as well. From a noise standpoint, snow is seldom quiet, unless it's in the form of fresh powder, or if it's rapidly thawing. Snow that has been on the ground for more than a few hours may be extremely noisy, and you can count on it being more noisy as the air temperature drops. Trying to walk on crusted snow that you break through every few steps is almost always an exercise in futility, as far as sneaking up to a deer is concerned.

Very dry weather is never appreciated because of the noise factor if the forest floor you're hunting on is covered with leaves. They will crunch maddeningly underneath your boots, and there's nothing you can do about it. In that case, stillhunting may not be an option; your best bet might be to try other techniques such as driving (if you're with a group of other hunters), or quietly watching from a stand, hoping deer will come by your location, either in the course of their daily travels or by being pushed by other hunters.

CLOTHING. Because of the need to move quietly, it's necessary to wear clothes that aren't noisy. Many new garments have waterproof features that render them stiff and noisy, and some are simply made of material that doesn't allow quiet walking. My choice has always been wool, because it's noiseless and is an excellent material in wet weather, though there are exceptions. I recall a muskox hunt in the arctic when my traditional and dependable woolen garments soaked up so much moisture that I felt like a sponge. On the other hand, I recall a blacktail hunt in western Washington when it rained 3 inches one day and my wool held up well. If you decide on non-woolen clothing, check out many of the new apparel items that are quiet as well as waterproof. It's always a good idea to touch the garment before purchasing

it, since you can literally determine its noise factor by scratching it with your fingernails. Of course, that's not possible if you order from a catalog. If you can, shop at a reputable sporting goods store that carries a wide selection of clothing. Nowadays, there are many large outlets offering a wide selection of different garments, such as the Cabela's and Bass Pro stores that are showing up everywhere.

GEAR. Because you're trying to spot a deer before it sees you, suitable optics are essential. I like 8 power binoculars, and I use them constantly. Because you're moving about, lightweight binoculars will be more comfortable to carry. I use a daypack to carry all the gear I'll need, and my preference is for a daypack that's been broken in and a good fit. See the section in this book on the special gear I carry in my daypack.

THE MENTAL ASPECT. Stillhunting cannot be successful if your brain isn't tuned to seeing and penetrating the vegetation around you. Concentration is all-important. You must literally force yourself to pay attention to the objective of spotting an animal, instead of thinking about a problem at home or the office. To be sure, many deer simply cannot be seen first, no matter how hard you try. Screening brush may conceal them from your view, especially if they're bedded and motionless. Since you're moving, and making noise, no matter how hard you try to be quiet, they'll undoubtedly spot you and make a hasty exit. But many of those animals may be in a position where they can't see you, though parts of their bodies are indeed visible. Any horizontal object or off-color patch should be suspect. Sometimes if a buck is positioned just right you can see an antler, or part of it, especially if the sun is reflecting off it.

TIMING. The best times to stillhunt are early and late in the day, when animals are up on their feet and moving between bedding and feeding areas. It's far easier to see a walking deer than one that's bedded, which is typically the case during the day. A bedded animal isn't just hunkered down where it's hard to see; it's also at high alert and keenly focused on the landscape around it. A dozing deer never lets its guard down, but will be at full attention at the slightest sound or scent.

HUNTING PATTERN. If possible, when you've completed stillhunting the area, turn around and come back through, rather than taking a road or path along the perimeter on your return. Deer that you disturbed on your initial walk might be up on their feet and moving. It's human nature to think that once a human passes through an area, all the deer immediately vacate the place. I don't know how many times I've seen tracks in the snow where deer have literally walked in my footprints just minutes after I made them.

Hunting in Evergreen Forests

Hunting in softwood or evergreen forests, also called "black timber" in the West, can be the toughest of all the mule deer habitats because of the poor visibility and physical difficulty of negotiating the steep terrain and thick forests. These forests, made up largely of firs, pines and spruces, often have little food value, especially in timber stands where the canopy is so tight that the sunlight seldom hits the ground. In that case, muleys typically leave the shelter of the timber to find food elsewhere, much like elk that also may share that habitat.

The density of trees in an evergreen forest depends on the species and age of trees, soil, climate, directional exposure and other factors. For example, ponderosa pines, which grow throughout much of the muley's range, typically grow in fairly sparse stands when they're overmature, with plenty of grass and underbrush on the forest floor. Lodgepole pine, on the other hand, grows in extremely thick stands, often called "doghair thickets," where there is little food available. Douglas fir may grow in pure stands where trees aren't as densely spaced as in lodgepole forests, and alpine fir and spruce may grow in old overmature forests where thick branches grow close to the ground.

WHERE TO FIND MULE DEER IN EVERGREENS

My favorite strategy of hunting these forests is to standhunt by watching potential feeding areas adjacent to thick timberstands. I use that method early and late in the day when deer are traveling from feeding to bedding areas and vice versa. Many evergreen forests are bordered by patches of brush such as scrub oak, serviceberry, mountain mahogany and other preferred plants. Deer need walk only a short distance from the timber to feed, and aren't exposed for any length of time.

In most cases, recently logged-over evergreen forests are hotspots for locating feeding deer. Because logging activity removes trees and the ground is disturbed, new shrubs and forbs quickly take root. The area becomes a virtual smorgasbord for deer, attracting animals for miles. It's a documented fact that logging enhances habitat from the standpoint of quickly producing quality forage.

Since logging is widely practiced on national forests, plenty of public land is available to hunters. Many roads leading to logged areas are closed, which offers an opportunity for a quality experience. Hunters willing to walk a few miles on these roads won't be disturbed by ATV's, pick-up trucks or large numbers of hunters. Some of my most memorable mule deer hunts were in and around thick evergreen forests where I'd hike in on a closed road and find plenty of deer in clearcuts. It amazes me how many people are unwilling to walk much more than a mile from a vehicle.

Old burns are also magnets for muleys, drawing them in to the succulent vegetation engendered by fires. As soon as a forest fire goes out, seeds immediately begin to sprout, and in no time the burned area is covered with high-quality nutritional forage. Fires that burn quickly through a forest are most beneficial because the humus layer in the ground isn't harmed. This type of fine occurs when a high wind pushes the flames through the tree crowns, and the fire doesn't eat away into the valuable top few inches of the forest floor. When the wind isn't a factor, the fire moves more slowly, consuming the upper layers of the soil. In that case, regeneration of a new forest is much slower because of the lack of soil nutrients.

In the cases of clearcuts and old burns, it's important to remember that the new growth eventually goes through a succession of species to the point where a new forest of evergreens becomes dominant and the valuable forage species disappear, overtopped by trees that once again block out the sunlight. Typically, the first 5 to 10 years after logging or a fire are best for attracting muleys, but that depends on many factors. Forest officers can tell you where recent clearcuts and burns are located. Your scouting efforts should include these places in your search for feeding areas.

In many mountainous areas, rimrock ledges run along ridges above evergreen forests. Bucks are fond of bedding in this country where they can see and hear danger above and below them. Whenever rimrock is present, I like to sneak along slowly, looking into small brushy pockets and around large boulders, especially on the shaded side. Because you're usually above the deer, you need to take pains not to be skylined. I like to move along just below the ridge, easing around the rocks and trees at a snail's pace, and always searching for a bedded deer. Since you're either on or close to ridges, be careful when shooting at a skylined deer. Always be sure your backstop is safe.

In places where there is a distinct timberline delineation, you'll often see a stunted forest of firs and spruces. These are windblown trees, seldom much more than 10 feet high, that grow on shallow soils where the growing season is a matter of a few weeks because of the severe weather at those elevations. Bucks commonly bed in these thickets – often referred to as krummholz forest – many of which aren't much more than an acre, and are surrounded by open tundra composed of ground willow. More than once I've jumped big wary bucks from these very dense thickets. Because of the high altitude and lack of nearby roads, deer are comfortable using these dwarf forests.

Because of the dense timber in most evergreen forests, deer are more apt to stick to major trails. In places where hunter traffic is heavy, it's a wise idea to watch trails all day long, especially if the trail leads into an especially dense blowdown, or into a steep canyon.

Since there's little forage in many evergreen forests, remember to look for natural movement of deer as they travel about early and late in the day. Use your binoculars constantly, and keep your scope at a lower power if it's a variable because you'll likely get a close-in shot.

Hunting in Pinyon-Juniper

Sprawling forests of pinyon pines and junipers blanket much of the lower elevations in mule deer country. To the uninformed, these forests don't "look" like mule deer habitat, because traditional muley country in the Rockies is more mountainous and at higher elevations. That being the case, hunters often drive through these lowland regions to get to

areas they believe are more productive. In some states, however, such as Nevada, Arizona and New Mexico, pinyon-juniper is the primary habitat, period, and hunters have no choice.

The forests, commonly known as the "cedars" or "PJ," typically grow in arid regions where there is little water. The soil that supports them is not terribly fertile, and is often covered with shale rock. Forage plants are usually absent, requiring deer to move out on a daily basis, feeding in adjacent areas such as sagebrush and high-desert habitats.

Hunting the PJ habitat is one of the toughest of all. Visibility is poor, travel is noisy, and you're essen-

tially looking for bedded animals that are extremely alert, though early in the morning and late in the afternoon you'll have an opportunity with animals walking to and from feeding areas.

The trees have branches that grow low to the ground, preventing decent visibility. Furthermore, the branches and foliage are "stiff," adding even more noise when you try to move about.

TECHNIQUES FOR HUNTING PINYON-JUNIPER

Of all the hunting techniques possible, standing and driving are often the most productive. Tracking, stalking and stillhunting are usually next to impossible because of the noise factor.

I can recall countless times when I've been frustrated at my inability to sneak close to deer. Loose, broken shale rock and twigs and branches usually betray my presence. Every now and then I'll successfully move within range of a good buck, and I fondly recall each of those incidents, numbering less than a dozen. Most of my successful hunts in the PJ were the result of watching waterholes and feeding areas, and putting on drives with groups of pals.

An effective technique, and my favorite, is to hunt a small draw where you can walk on top of the ridge and see the opposing ridge and part of that slope. The idea is to jump a deer in the draw or either slope, and spot it as it runs away from you up the opposite ridge. If all works in your favor, a buck will flush and show itself where you can get a shot. Often the deer will stop at a high spot to see what spooked it.

Driving muleys in the PJ works best if you select a small area to hunt. If you try to drive a large area, too much country is available for the animals to escape in. Pick a place that has plenty of deer sign and is completely or partially surrounded by open sagebrush areas.

If you want to try stand hunting, forget treestands. The gnarly, twisted trees festooned with branches offer no way to use a self-climber, and a stand previously erected will offer little advantage in the way of visibility because of the foliage. In fact, the best position to hunt from is on the ground, getting low where you can see under the branches.

You'll notice plenty of trails through the PJ, many of them creating a confusing network where you'll be hard put to determine which are most likely being used. Of course, snow will help you figure deer movements in the maze if snow is present. To ambush a deer on a trail, you'll need to be in place very early in the morning and late in the afternoon. In both cases you'll no doubt be traveling in the dark.

Waterholes offer an ambush option, but seldom a successful one because muleys often travel to water in the night, especially if there is the slightest bit of hunting pressure. You can find hidden water sources by talking to ranchers, sheepherders, foresters, range specialists and other people familiar with the area you're hunting. Much of the PJ habitat is on land administered by the U.S. government, notably the BLM. By talking to personnel in those offices, you can also gain an insight into water sources.

The PJ forest varies in density. Some forests have very tightly woven canopies; others have more of an open environment. Older bucks will bed in the heavier areas, because of the security cover. It's virtually impossible to spot them before they see or hear you, and a drive is the only option. More open areas are best hunted by moving along slowly and looking for animals bedded in the shade.

Tracking in the snow might be possible if the snow is soft and quiet, and the wind is in your favor. Success, as always in the PJ, is typically dependent on the noise factor.

Some of my very best muleys have been taken in the PJ country. Not only does this habitat harbor big bucks, it may have far less hunting pressure in places where hunters have an option of hunting higher country. To many, the vast PJ forests of the West don't seem to have the potential of supporting deer. That's exactly the reason you should hunt there.

The Clearing Connection

On hundreds of thousands of acres of pinyon-juniper (most of it federal BLM land), a unique land-clearing method has been practiced. In order to engender the growth of forage plants, the forest is literally torn down by a huge ship-anchor chain connected to two bulldozers. The machines drag the chain, which tears the trees out of the ground. The trees are later piled into large rows and either burned or left alone. Immediately afterward, seeds from desirable forage species are sown, and if all goes well, a cornucopia of wonderful grasses and forbs spring forth to provide feed for livestock and wildlife. This practice, mostly done in the 60s and 70s, has since become highly controversial, since many environmental organizations view it as too destructive and harmful to some endangered and threatened species. Chained openings are ideal places to watch for feeding deer early in the morning and late in the afternoon, especially if you must hike in to them. Other hotspots in the PJ forests are old burns. As in the case of the chained areas, these too offer plenty of food to muleys.

Hunting in Aspens

A good share of mule deer country is in the West's most glorious landscape. In the fall, quaking aspens light up the mountain slopes in a spectacular panorama of color that would rival New England's famous maples.

Geographically, aspens are most prevalent in the central Rockies. Colorado, Utah, southern Idaho and southern Wyoming have the bulk of them, though there are extensive forests in parts of Nevada, New Mexico and other states.

As October approaches, and with it the general mule deer seasons in most of the western states, the aspen foliage falls, blanketing the forest floor with several inches of crunchy leaves. Bowhunters are afield in September when the trees are brilliantly colored, but firearms hunters often see a naked forest in mid-October. This is for the better, since visibility is far greater, allowing deer to be seen as they travel about.

Aspens grow in mid-elevation ranges, from 6,000 to 9,000 feet or more. They may be in pure stands, or mixed with conifers. In some areas, aspens grow in draws and on ridges, surrounded by wide expanses of sagebrush, scrub oak and other low-growing shrubs.

Since undergrowth in these forests may be lush, deer often remain in this cover without leaving, unless water is absent. In that case, animals may walk 2 or 3 miles to water, which may be located in waterholes maintained for livestock. Cattle trails may be well defined in aspen country, allowing hunters to slip along quietly, unless freshly fallen leaves have not yet been soaked by a good rain or snow. If not, silent walking in the forest might be out of the question.

The best hunting techniques in aspens are usually spot and stalk, and stillhunting. I like to climb to a high ridge, or drive out on a ridge in my pickup and hike as far as I can from roads. I usually have a vantage point in mind, and I want to be there well before daybreak, which means a walk in the dark. My observation spot will offer a commanding view of several slopes, where I can see into many drainages.

WHERE TO START

To begin the day, I put the binoculars to work as soon as the gray light preceding dawn affords the least bit of visibility. I look for deer in sagebrush and other brushy areas first, since that's where they're apt to forage during the night. Later, I'll slowly scan the trees for deer moving from feeding to bedding areas.

Muleys may bed in the aspen forest, or travel out to spend the day in a patch of brush. This is often the case where oak brush thickets are mingled with the trees. Whenever I spot deer moving in the morning, my first order of business is to determine if a suitable buck is among them. If so, I watch intently to determine where they might be headed. By observing their movements, I try to set up an ambush by easing through the forest with the wind in my favor. I pick a spot from my vantage point and work my way to it. If you're hunting with a companion, it's a good idea to have your pal watch the deer as you move or vice versa. More than once the quarry had bedded down before I got to my ambush spot, and I didn't know it because I was out of sight. If that's the case, your partner can then direct you to the deer with hand signals. A word about ethics here: many hunters are using two-way radios these days. That might be okay to signal a pal to help get a deer out, or to call in an emergency, but it's never okay to use an electronic device to guide a hunter to game. In my book that's immoral and unethical, and it should be illegal in every state.

If deer are feeding in the trees or in brushy places in the perimeter of the forest, I'll waste no time putting on a stalk. Muleys may bed down very early, many times before the sun reaches the eastern horizon.

Bitterly cold mornings may be possible. If that's the case, don't make the mistake of glassing for deer only in sunny spots. We typically give animals human qualities, believing that if it's cold, they'll head for the sun to warm up. In fact the reverse is often true. Deer have warm pelts, and are more comfortable and secure in shadier spots than in the sun, regardless of the temperature.

Competition from other hunters may be intense in aspen forests, especially along accessible roads in public areas. If that's the case, put as much distance you can between you and the nearest road, and leave camp early to get the jump on everyone else. Use other hunters to your advantage by being situated in a good spot when others are just beginning to leave the roads.

One of my favorite areas to hunt is an aspen forest where deep, brushy draws run down between valleys. The brush is so thick that traveling deer are practically invisible, and most hunters have no clue the deer are using them. I like to find a spot in the aspens where the brush thins just enough to allow me to see animals.

Spooked deer may or may not use trails, so it's difficult to figure out how to intercept them. I like to be on a ridge where I can be very mobile, moving quickly to get a shot at deer heading for escape cover.

During a Colorado hunt, I drove by no less than 15 camps in the dark, and drove to the end of a logging road that was blocked by a gate. I parked there and walked a mile up the road, then turned off on a high ridge and walked another half mile into a large aspen forest. I picked a vantage point where I knew other hunters would soon be moving about. I left camp at 4 a.m. to pull this off, because I wanted to be in place long before people started stirring. Before shooting light I began to see orange-clad hunters moving in the distance off the roads, and soon I saw deer moving about, nervously evading people. Shooting light was barely 5 minutes old when I put down a dandy four-point buck that was running with three other bucks. When I fired, he was looking at two hunters headed in his direction; the deer never knew I was in his world.

I particularly like stillhunting in aspens because deer like bedding there, so there are plenty of animals about. The type of vegetation in the forest also allows you to move within cover at all times, enabling you to be easily shielded if deer show up and walk into view. If the understory isn't terribly dense, it's not all that difficult to spot a bedded buck before it sees you.

Land ownership in aspen country is often private in valley bottoms where homesteaders staked their claims. However, literally millions of acres are in national forests, and other huge blocks are administered by the Bureau of Land Management. Public hunting is insured, but some of the best hunting may be on private land where there is less hunting pressure.

Roads may be extensive in aspen forests, many of them constructed years ago by the government for the benefit of livestock operators. In some national forests, there's a road on every major ridge and along every big valley. That being the case, hunters flock to aspen country, since plenty of deer as well as livestock are fond of this habitat. Hunting aspens requires you to hunt smart, because plenty of other folks will be trying to tag the same big buck that you are. The effort is worth it, because plenty of big bucks come from aspen country every year.

Hunting in Sagebrush

Vast regions of the West are covered with expansive areas of sagebrush. Tens of millions of acres of this plant community grow in our western states. This, if it can be said of any of the diverse habitats, is the traditional land of the mule deer. With few exceptions, find sagebrush and you'll find muleys.

This plant has many varieties, some of which are more palatable to deer than others. But only a scientist knows which is which, meaning that we hunters see sage as an all-inclusive form of vegetation. Some sagebrush is

very tall, especially where soils are fertile and well-drained. Other forms are short, eking out an existence in high deserts where precipitation is very low.

Muleys depend on sagebrush for a large part of their winter diet. It's a critical item, and can cause an entire mule deer herd to crash if it's in short supply due to drought, severe winters or overgrazing.

Hunting in sagebrush country can be an enlightening experience to people who are used to pursuing deer in wooded areas. The lack of trees is a foreign sight;

many newcomers to this country would swear it's devoid of deer.

My first mule deer hunt was in sagebrush country, where deep canyons wound through rolling hills and emptied into cedar forests in lower elevations. My host drove me to my stand in one of those canyons before sunup, and I had no idea what to expect. I hadn't been in that area before, having arrived at camp during the night. As the upcoming dawn offered increasing glimpses of the landscape, I was amazed to see no trees. Surely, I thought, no deer could possibly live in that country. Mind you, I was raised in the East, accustomed to hunting whitetails in oak and hickory forests.

Imagine my astonishment when I spotted a huge buck walking in the bottom of the canyon soon after sunrise. I put him down, and was amazed at not only his body size and antlers, but the fact that he dwelled in this strange land of seemingly endless sagebrush. That buck, my first muley ever, taken in 1961, field-dressed at 235 pounds. Since then, I've taken many more bucks in the sage, and now see the environment as a prime chunk of mule deer country.

Sagebrush habitat is typically easily accessed because of its often gentle lowland terrain, and hunting pressure is commonly very heavy. Deer are quickly driven out of high human traffic areas, taking refuge in surrounding country that offers more security, or in patches of high, dense brush that grows within the sage environment. That brush is often called "buck brush," and usually consists of serviceberry, scrub oak, mountain mahogany or a combination of those.

Astute hunters will approach those dense brush patches as if every one held a deer or two, and be ready for a quick shot. In places where stands might be several acres, a drive will often rout muleys into the open.

Don't overlook small washes, also called gullies or coulees, that run through the open sage. I recall an incident where I once came upon a tiny gully hardly 6 feet wide and 4 feet deep, containing an enormous quantity of tumbleweed. Acting on a hunch, I tossed sticks and rocks in, and was about to walk away when a buck boiled out and bounced off through the countryside.

In places where deer aren't disturbed by humans, they'll likely bed in the sage itself, even if the sage isn't much more than 2 feet high. For that reason, always be on guard when hiking into small pockets and basins. Just because you don't see deer doesn't mean they aren't close by. When deer are surprised by hunters, they may very well hide and remain in their beds. All you can see is the tips of their antlers.

TIPS FOR HUNTING IN SAGEBRUSH

It's a wise idea, as always, but especially in open sagebrush, to be well into the hunting area long before daylight. I like to find a high vantage point where I can literally see miles of sage around me, and begin glassing as soon as I can see. Many times I'll spot feeding deer, and will actually watch them bed down. By doing so, I have the rest of the day to plan a strategy. More than once I've stalked within range of unsuspecting bedded deer that I observed from a distance.

Even where hunting pressure is heavy, you can find bucks by simply driving to the end of the road and hiking off into broken country where few other hunters go. I've found that most people won't walk much more than a mile or two, if that. Because of the openness of the terrain, many hunters tend to road hunt or make short forays from their vehicle. That's a big mistake, because deer are often just out of sight a short distance from a road where people don't bother to look. Once, my son and I were hunting in Colorado, and hadn't seen many deer in the places most other folks hunted. We walked just a half mile to a canyon that was thick with serviceberry, and sat there until dark. Dan took a good buck that had evidently been bedded in the high brush, and I saw a beauty that I couldn't get a shot at.

Binoculars are a must in hunting this open land, and a spotting scope is a good idea, too. So is some sort of a rest that you can use to steady your rifle, because there are few items to use as a rest in the low sage. If nothing else is available, I'll quickly plop my hat on top of a bush and settle my rifle into the hat.

It's important to remember that bucks that were born and raised in sagebrush country may be reluctant to leave it. They're used to the openness and high visibility. This is worth repeating: sometimes all it takes is to make a short hike off the beaten path, as I did recently in eastern Oregon. I followed a small buck through the sage to a point where he topped out over a rise. When I got to the ridge where he disappeared, I was astounded to see five big bedded bucks staring at me from a distance of 400 yards. They were barely out of sight of the road, and felt secure in their bedding area. As it was, they whistled out of there before I could come up with a stalk strategy.

Don't ignore the millions of acres of sagebrush country in the West. Much of it is productive and home to some dandy muleys.

Hunting in High Brush

Perhaps the toughest mule deer hunting is in thick stands of high brush, particularly scrub oak, commonly called oak brush, which thrives in the central Rockies, mostly in Colorado, Utah, New Mexico, Wyoming and Idaho. This plant, which is typically 6 to 8 feet high, may reach 12 feet or more on good soil. It has the nasty ability to grow in very dense stands, some of which practically defy human travel. That's exactly why deer love it and you should hunt it.

But how? Seeing deer in this thick vegetation takes some doing. Occasionally you'll spot them if you're on a high opposing ridge and can look down. In stands where there are clearings, you might see deer traveling about and feeding in the open.

Oak stands typically have plenty of forage, especially during years of heavy mast production. Even during lean years, muleys will munch on oak twigs and vegetation that grows within and around the brush. In addition, the security offered by the thickets is extremely attractive to deer, and animals will travel long distances to bed in them.

STRATEGIES FOR HUNTING IN HIGH BRUSH

My preferred strategy is to initially scout oak country prior to the season, checking for fresh sign, but that isn't always an indication of deer activity when the season opens. Many seemingly barren areas may support plenty of deer after the season opens, since the heavy cover offers a sanctuary from hunters. Deer will commonly abandon their normal haunts and head for the security of high brush as soon as they feel threatened by increased human activity.

I like to hike up to a high vantage point where I can look down into oak cover. Many times this brush will grow adjacent to aspen stands, and deer will travel from the aspens to the oaks early in the morning. By finding a good vantage point before shooting light, I can watch for deer movement, and then try to set up an ambush. If you see deer enter the oak brush, it's usually too late to make a move, but you at least know the precise location of deer for the rest of the day, since they'll no doubt bed in the oaks. That being the case, you can set up a drive and try to move deer

out, but be aware they won't come out easily, especially if the patch is much larger than 4 or 5 acres.

I won't attempt to put on a drive in large oak thickets if I'm looking for a big buck. I've tried it too many times, and it simply won't work, usually because deer are hesitant to exit the safety of the thicket. They'll slip and ease around in the cover, seldom seen by humans. It's best to push smaller patches where standers can see potential escape points. Deer will usually exit a brush patch via a small connecting finger of brush, or will head for steep, rugged country adjacent to the oaks, if they leave at all.

Stillhunting in oak brush can be a futile effort unless you're working a spot that's sparsely vegetated where you can look into openings. The best time to try this is early in the morning and late in the afternoon when deer are up and about. Trying to spot them when they're bedded is almost impossible. There's almost always an unavoidable noise factor in the oaks because of the leaf litter. If it's raining and the wind is blowing, you can get away with quieter travel, but be sure you're wearing clothing that isn't inherently noisy.

There are species of vegetation in the high brush other than scrub oak, notably mountain mahogany, serviceberry and other species. All offer plenty of concealment to muleys, and for that reason they'll always be hot spots. If you can't find a buck anywhere else, the high brush should be your last resort – or your first, depending on how you look at it.

A nice aspect of hunting thick brush is the simple fact that you won't have much company. In mule deer country overrun with hordes of hunters, that's plenty of reason to suffer a bit and hunt the dense thickets.

Don't Lose Your Buck

Always carry some orange flagging tape with you when you hunt any heavy brush, especially in scrub oak country where everything looks the same. The tape will help you locate your deer if you need to return to it. I almost lost a big buck once because the single marker (some toilet tissue) blew down. I looked a long time for the deer when I returned and almost didn't find it prior to dark.

Hunting in River Bottoms

Many rivers course through prime mule deer country, offering several hunting strategies, the most unique being actually floating the river and hunting as you move downstream.

Typical western rivers, such as the Missouri, Yellowstone, Snake, Salmon, Green and Colorado, begin as brawling watercourses, but many settle down and meander peacefully though lowland elevations. In the case of wild rapids and waves, you absolutely must be thoroughly skilled in whitewater rafting. In many areas, where the river flows through public land, you may need a permit from the appropriate government agency. Where the river runs more peacefully, you'll encounter few, if any serious rapids. Cottonwood trees are the primary dominant tree species in the lower country, and either willow or tamarisk makes up much of the understory. Muleys are common in all parts of most rivers, but in some places you'll see more whitetails, and in other places

raft will nicely accommodate two people, a six-man raft three). It's also a good idea, and in fact almost mandatory, to have an extra raft to haul gear and of course the big bucks you expect to take. For obvious reasons, stow your gear in waterproof containers. A cell phone is a good idea in case you have unexpected problems and need assistance. Most river hunts are more than one-day trips, which means you'll probably camp along shore.

Be sure you have an updated map because most rivers flow through private as well as public land. Time your float so you can camp where you intend to make your evening and morning hunt. In places where the vegetation is fairly thick, muleys will often bed in the understory, offering an ideal drive strategy. One technique that works is to let off a hunter or two, and then float downriver to a point where the other hunter can find a vantage point. A small drive may rout deer to waiting standers. In areas where deer are moving from river bottoms to feeding areas, and vice versa, be on stand before shooting light in a spot where you can watch trails. Likewise, do the same thing in late afternoon.

Be quiet as you float, since deer may be bedded close to the water's edge. If you encounter islands that have brushy cover, don't overlook them, because they're favorite safety havens for muleys. Remember that deer are good swimmers, and may try to escape via a water route.

In places the river may be bordered by low cliffs or high rises of land, allowing an opportunity to watch from an elevated vantage point. In some areas you can select a spot and see for extremely long distances. Portable treestands work well in places where there are well-defined trails but no high spots in which to observe muleys.

Floating a river isn't only fun, it also offers hunters the mobility to move quickly from one location to another. Another advantage is the relatively low numbers of hunters where the river isn't accessible via roads. Deer aren't disturbed as they normally would be, and their behavior patterns are determined fairly easily.

Many western rivers are dammed, forming large reservoirs. This is another opportunity to use water as a hunting medium, but in this case you need a boat that will transport you to areas where there are few hunters. The advantage here is being able to find a secluded spot where there's less hunting pressure. Some very big bucks live within a mile of the shoreline, and relatively few are disturbed because hunters are simply absent. This is the chief reason to use a raft or a boat. Because of the transportation and logistical problems involved, only a few hunters go to the trouble of hunting this way. That's exactly why you should give it a try.

only whitetails. It's obvious that you need to do some homework when planning your trip.

FLOAT HUNTING OPTIONS

To float a river, you'll need to solve a logistical problem. You put your craft and gear in at one point, but you must already have made arrangements for someone to pick you up at your destination spot, or at least have a vehicle waiting for you there. Ideally, three people are optimum for a hunt like this. You'll fit comfortably in an eight-man raft. (For some strange reason, rafts are classified by dividing the occupancy number in half to get the actual load – a four-man

Hunting in the Desert

There's some confusion over desert mule deer and mule deer that live in the desert. According to some authorities, there is a very definite desert mule deer subspecies. But then comes along wildlife expert Dr. Valerius Geist, who states in his book, *Deer of the World*, "The desert mule deer is not a valid subspecies."

Early in this book all the mule deer subspecies were discussed, but for the purposes of this chapter we'll address mule deer that inhabit either the "hot" or "high deserts" in North America. I define a "hot" desert as a low-elevation environment such as you might find in California, west Texas, Mexico, etc. A "high" desert would be a habitat at 6,000 feet or more that you might find in Colorado, Utah, Wyoming and other similar regions. Both of these deserts are characterized by very hardy plants that can exist with low amounts of precipitation such as greasewood, saltbush, chaparral and others. The lack of water and excessive summer heat are also distinctive factors in a desert environment.

WHERE TO FIND DESERT MULEYS

Mule deer normally don't have high populations in the desert for obvious reasons. Quality food is comparatively scarce, water is usually scattered over wide locations, and the lack of cover is conducive to predator assaults, especially on fawns.

Because of low densities, muleys are often overlooked in this seemingly hostile environment. Astute hunters who know better often go home with a wide smile – and a huge buck.

Without question the biggest desert bucks of North America come from the state of Sonora in Mexico. These animals have huge, wide, massive antlers, and impress everyone who views them. The hunting strategy is unique, and is probably done exclusively in Sonora and places like it. You'll be following a guide who speaks little or no English, and he'll search the desert until he finds the track of a big buck. From that point on, you'll dog that specific animal, perhaps for days, until you ultimately catch up to it or lose the track. If you catch up, you'll jump the deer, and be offered with only a snap shot opportunity. If you blow the shot, you continue to follow, or track another buck. The role of the guide is obvious. This man will undoubtedly have the uncanny ability to track a deer in unbelievable country, and you'll marvel at his skills. On the negative side, these hunts have now become very expensive because of the quality of bucks being taken, and even worse, some Mexican outfitters are offering high-dollar hunts in areas that have few or no quality deer. The almighty dollar obviously has caused some people to trade integrity for money.

But for those of us who choose to hunt mule deer in western deserts, there are some very definite strategies that work better than others. One of the most obvious is watching a waterhole, especially in very arid areas where water is scattered far and wide. I think that's a mistake, and often a waste of time. First, there are often small seeps and springs that deer use, including many hidden and unknown to hunters. I realized just how many seeps a very arid region can have while hunting desert bighorn sheep several years ago. I came across places where just a bit of water issued forth between rocks, usually in a canyon or ravine. Deer and sheep tracks were everywhere, and I wouldn't have discovered the water unless I stumbled into it, as I had done. Second, muleys may walk miles to water, so you won't necessarily find them close by. Third, mule deer quite often go to water only in the darkness, so waiting for them to show up during shooting hours isn't a good option. And finally, deer may not water for days. In some dry areas, mule deer are conditioned to obtaining much of their water needs through the vegetation they eat, and free water isn't a daily requirement.

For all those reasons, keying on a waterhole may not be a wise idea, but I believe that using the water as a central point from which to hunt is prudent. I like to hunt the most rugged desert country I can find within 4 of 5 miles of water. In desert areas, buttes and rocky ridges jut high over the desert floor. Big bucks will often bed in those spots where they have a commanding view and can see for a mile or more. Old deer will also find refuge in patches of thick brush, such as greasewood or saltbrush. This vegetation often grows in and around washes, also called arroyos or coulees.

My favorite strategy when hunting the desert is to park the vehicle long before shooting light and hike to a high spot. It's tempting to drive around and look for deer because of the very open country, but a smart buck will see and or hear you coming a long way off and be long gone before you can get out and make the shot. Hike to the top of a rimrock escarpment where you can see a long way in every direction and use your glasses effectively.

Don't assume that deer will only bed in and around patches of brush. On many instances I've jumped big bucks in places that astounded me. They were in spots with little or no cover, but in almost every case they were in out-of-the-way places where few hunters looked. And that's the key, any animal will seek a place where it feels secure. That's exactly why they're there.

Hunting in Agricultural Areas

Muleys are quite at home on farms and ranches, though their presence is dictated largely by migration patterns. In some areas, mule deer remain permanent residents around ranches, and in others they make a part-time appearance in the fall when snow drives them out of the mountains. They remain in lower elevations until spring, when they can once again access their high summer ranges.

Preferred foods are alfalfa and various grasses, though muleys also forage on practically all grain crops. Where deer numbers are heavy enough, significant damage is done to croplands, and muleys become liabilities. In that case, there's more incentive to hunt them. Generous numbers of antlerless tags may be offered to keep the herds trimmed.

Of course, ranches and farms are privately owned, though there are some state lands and federal refuges where agricultural practices are conducted for wildlife. By and large, however, you'll be dealing with private landowners, and chances are good you won't be allowed to hunt for free.

Many private lands are leased these days. Outfitters and groups of hunters have essentially tied up much prime mule deer country in the West. The only way to hunt those places is to join one of those groups, or hire an outfitter. There are still some ranches that can be hunted for free, but you might have to look long and hard to find them. Landowners have discovered that the wildlife that lives on their property can bring in revenue, and logically pursue those avenues where the highest dollars can be obtained.

Back in the early 60s, when I first ventured west to study forestry, I could knock on practically any rancher's door and get permission to hunt for free. The landowner was usually friendly, offering a cup of coffee and even an occasional piece of homemade pie. His only concern was that I close gates behind me, keep off fragile roads when it was wet, and stay away from pastures that contained livestock. It's a sad commentary on our modern times that those days are gone forever.

Many ranches and farms are surrounded by federal or state land, offering excellent hunting opportunities

the mark; in another case about 250 yards. Today, with updated maps and reasonably priced GPS units, there's no excuse for straying onto private land. Whenever you hunt close to a boundary, be sure you take pains to know precisely where you are at all times. If there's a question, don't enter the area, even if there's plenty of deer sign.

MULE DEER TRAVEL ROUTES

Since deer typically visit the fields in the night, they'll start moving toward croplands late in the afternoon from bedding areas that can be as much as 3 or 4 miles away. It's a wise idea to scout those bedding areas as well as the edges of fields to determine the trails the deer are using. Better yet, watch the deer prior to the season opener so you can establish an ambush spot when the season arrives.

Deer may begin moving an hour or two before the sun sets, depending on the weather and other local conditions. You can usually assume the bigger bucks will be the last to arrive, and many times they'll show up well after dark. On several occasions I watched a field until the last second of shooting light. After I hiked back to my pickup, and drove past the field I'd watched, it wasn't uncommon for my headlights to pick up a huge buck or two in the field I'd been watching. Obviously the big boys waited until the light was gone before stepping out of cover.

You can reverse the strategy in the morning, setting up for deer returning from the fields. I've done this a number of times, and have been frustrated because the big bucks usually beat me back to their bed locations. Many times the wary animals will leave the croplands well before shooting light and are in their bedding areas in the dark. More than once I've jumped deer in the night when I was headed for an ambush spot. The best way to overcome this problem is to slip into a bedding area that's far from the fields. That way, you'll encounter deer moving during shooting hours.

Hunting around ranches and farms that contain visible deer in fields may require you to deal with other hunters. The feeding animals will attract plenty of attention, and other people will have their eyes on those deer as well. A couple years ago I hunted Utah's famed Paunsagaunt unit, renowned for its huge muleys. On the opener I set up at a vantage point on public land overlooking a field that a giant buck had been feeding in. I was dismayed to find that a half dozen other hunters had the same idea. The buck was nowhere to be seen, which came as no surprise.

Farmland bucks are perhaps the most predictable because their patterns appear to be simple, but don't let that lull you into thinking they're easy. You'll have to hunt smart and hard to outwit them.

on those neighboring acres. Typically, deer feed in the fields during the evening hours, and then travel to bedding spots in adjacent brushy areas. In many instances, those bedding areas are federal lands, open to public hunting.

Before you charge out and stake a claim on federal land in your attempt to ambush a buck, be sure you know exactly where the boundaries are. In many states, landowners aren't required to post their property. It's up to you to know exactly where you are. Of course, an updated map is required, and a GPS unit will pinpoint your location.

On two occasions in Wyoming, a state where posting land isn't required, my outdated maps caused me to hunt on private land where I had no permission. Those lands looked exactly like federal BLM lands, with plenty of sagebrush and prairie grass. No fence delineated the private land, and it was almost impossible to figure out where I was (this was before GPS instruments came on the scene). As it turned out, I was confronted by the landowners in each case, and as luck would have it, they were friendly chaps who gave me permission to hunt. They admitted that even they had difficulty pinpointing the boundaries of their property. In one case I was about 100 yards off

Coping with Crowds

Here's an unfortunate but common scenario. A group of hunters from an eastern state drive west for their first mule deer hunt. They're excited and ready for the hunt of their life, finally fulfilling a dream that they've long yearned for. But that dream becomes a nightmare when they discover unbelievable numbers of hunters everywhere they go. The only thing they can count on is millions of acres of public land where there are no posted signs. And that's exactly why the crowds are there. Plenty of people take advantage of the wide open and free spaces, but there's a price to pay for that freedom. The answer to avoiding crowds is to hunt private land where you'll probably have to

pay a hefty fee, or book with an outfitter, or draw a limited entry area. Those options might not be possible, leaving you at the mercy of the crowds.

Is there a way to beat the odds and still take a good buck, despite heavy hunting pressure? The answer is a resounding yes, but you'll have to hunt smart as well as put in a bit of effort. Every year, plenty of big bucks are taken by hunters where there are plenty of people about. Some of those hunters are lucky – being in the right place at the right time – and some of those are skilled – knowing how to hunt crafty muleys that are experts at hiding and surviving.

To take a big buck in crowded woods, you must look at the escape possibilities, and start there. Immediately rule out open country where there's good access. The big boys won't be there, having learned early on that high-visibility areas spell danger. That doesn't mean you must hike a dozen miles from a road to find a big buck. The key is the disturbance factor. If a buck feels

spots for two reasons. First, once you descend into the bottom of a steep canyon, you must hike back out at the end of the day. That physical effort alone will deter many people. Second, if you indeed get a buck in that nasty spot, you're faced with the dilemma of getting it out – with most of the route uphill. Thus, you'll often have those canyons to yourself. About the only competition will come from hunters who walk the rims and look down, hoping to spot a bedded deer. Those bucks will stay put, and won't move unless flushed by a hunter who approaches too close.

If no canyons are in your area, find a spot in the timber, whether it's aspen, fir or whatever, and stay there all day. The object here is to spot bucks being moved by other hunters. Choose your vantage point where active trails converge, especially if there's good visibility. Keep in mind that spooked deer may not run on the trails, but may dash through the forest. Resist the temptation to leave and go back to camp for lunch, because that might be the time the buck of your dreams will come by.

It's important to be at your vantage spot well before shooting light. Hunters will begin arriving early, and deer will immediately be pushed around. You want to be ready when the bucks are running. If you can find a spot near a large blowdown or thicket, stay there and keep watch. Those are perfect refuges for deer, since few people will hunt in them. Remember that the key to finding deer in a crowded situation is to recognize the places that they'll use for a sanctuary.

Don't underestimate the staying power of a smart muley. I learned that lesson when I watched a buck disappear in a small draw. I could see both ends, and was positive he didn't come out. After a half hour I descended the slope and began throwing rocks. The buck flushed after I'd tossed at least a dozen rocks within 10 yards of him.

Another time I jumped a dozen does, fawns and small bucks from an aspen-covered slope that was undergrown with heavy brush. Convinced that a big buck was still in there because of tracks I'd seen in the snow, I walked in and began making a racket. It took 5 minutes of making noise before he showed, and when he came out he was a blur of motion. He churned up an opposite slope and I put him down when he slowed near the top.

It's easy to be discouraged when the woods seem to be aglow with hunter orange. Don't despair, but remember that the bucks are still around. They'll be tougher to hunt, but with confidence and perseverance you can get the job done if you don't give up too soon. That big buck might very well show up when you least expect him to.

secure in a dense oak thicket that literally borders a heavily traveled road, he may very well use that patch of cover as a hiding area. Passing vehicles aren't a threat, but hunters who invade his sanctuary will force him out. If you recognize that cover as a potential hiding spot and put on a well-executed drive, your reward might very well be a big buck.

WHERE TO LOOK FOR PRESSURED BUCKS

Having said that, I think it's more characteristic for a mature buck to seek a safe haven in a place off the beaten track. If a deep canyon or gorge is anywhere within your hunt area, and there's no road in the bottom, that's the first place I'd look. Bucks love to hide in such places, especially if brush grows thick in the bottoms or on the slopes. I've found that deer will walk several miles to find such a place, traveling about in the darkness. Hunters normally shun those

THE WORD "TROPHY" will have a different meaning depending on the hunter.

Trophy Hunting

When you look at a picture of a live mule deer in a magazine, invariably you'll gaze at a splendid animal with outsized antlers. What you don't know is that wildlife photographers focus on the biggest bucks they can find, and many of them are in parks or refuges where they aren't hunted.

To the uninformed, mega-muleys abound in the West; all you need to do is to be a persistent, tough hunter, and you'll earn a big buck. Sadly, that's not the case. There are many areas in the West where there are no big bucks, either because of genes, poor quality food or the age factor.

But first let's define a trophy buck. The word "trophy" means many things to many people. When my daughter, Janette, shot her first buck many years ago, that little forkhorn became a memorable trophy to me, and it still is. Of all the hunts I've been on, that one ranks at the top. As they say, a trophy is in the eye of the beholder.

To most hunters, a trophy is simply an animal that engenders affection. It is proudly displayed on a wall, whether it's a buck with a modest spread, or one with outstanding antlers. To some, a buck earns more respect as a trophy if it was taken with some degree of difficulty, or if it was taken with a bow or blackpowder rifle. Believe it or not, one of my most memorable mule deer trophies was a big doe I'd taken with a bow after a tough pursuit.

TRUE TROPHIES ARE A RARE BREED

A 30-inch-wide outside spread is the measure which a trophy buck must have, in the eyes of many hunters. For some reason, the 30-inch figure is a magic number that either makes or breaks a buck's status. I have no idea where that measure originated, but it's firmly established. It's not uncommon in conversations among hunters to ask how many 30-inches another hunter has. When I was guiding mule deer hunters in the early 1960s, the 30-inch measure was well entrenched. Many of my hunters were bound and determined to take a 30-incher or go home empty-handed.

Unfortunately, there are plenty of places where 30-inch bucks don't exist, even among old bucks that have enough age to grow huge antlers. Genetics and quality feed are important factors that determine the mass and configuration of a buck's rack. There are indeed some places in the West where mega-bucks may be found, but there are far more where they can't. If I had my choice to hunt a huge muley, I'd look at southwest Wyoming, southeast Idaho, southern Utah, northern Arizona, and Nevada. That's not to say that you can't find a bruiser of a buck in Colorado, in Oregon, or even in western Kansas or Nebraska, because all those places have them. But some regions consistently produce more bigger deer than others.

The Boone and Crockett Club is the official scoring organization of North American big-game trophies. In order to make the minimum score to qualify in the book, a buck must score at least 190 in the typical category, and 230 in the non-typical category.

In the most current record book, there are almost 700 typical listings, and more than 500 non-typical listings. To put a buck in the record book, you'll need to be extremely fortunate. Perhaps lucky is a better word. Very few record-book bucks are taken by serious trophy hunters; by far the majority are killed by people who simply are at the right place at the right time. It makes sense to peruse the book carefully to determine where the trophies are coming from if you're serious about hunting a spot with good potential. But be sure to look at the dates the animals were taken, since many places that historically produced record bucks are no longer doing so. I believe 1990 would be a good cutoff date, since bucks taken after that reflect a more accurate picture of current potential.

Bowhunters may enter their mule deer trophies in the Pope and Young Club record book, which has lower minimum requirements for obvious reasons. It's far more difficult to take a larger animal with a bow than with a firearm. Blackpowder hunters also have a record keeping organization, called the Longhunter Society.

Most organizations use a scoring system that recognize balance or symmetry as the key factor when measuring animals. This is a quality assessment, giving animals with the most perfect heads the highest scores. In this case, "perfect" refers to a rack that has similar antlers on each side. After each antler is measured, the difference between the measurements is deducted from the final score. For example, say the brow tine on the right antler is 5 inches, and the brow tine on the left antler is 4 inches. The difference between the two is 1 inch, which is then subtracted from the total score. And so on for each other individual measurements.

When assessing a rack for trophy status, look for a long main beam, deep forks, a wide inside spread between main beams, long brow tines and plenty of mass all around. Use the chart in this book as a guideline to help you evaluate the key measurements that determine trophy status. If you think you have a buck that might make the record book, contact your local wildlife agency and inquire as to where you might locate an official measurer. The rack cannot be officially scored until 60 days after the animal was killed, and the rack must dry naturally in the air during that period.

Before your western hunt, bone up on what an actual muley looks like by checking out mounted heads. Pay a visit to a taxidermy shop, or a local sporting goods store where heads are displayed. Try to size up the antlers with parts of the head. For example, the ears of an alert buck will measure from 18 to 22 inches from tip to tip, or possibly a bit longer for a bigger buck. It's important to remember that to make this comparison, the buck must be looking directly at you. If his head is angled a bit, you won't be able to tell. Therefore, if a muley is staring at you and his antlers extend 4 or 5 inches outside his ear tips, slip your safety off and let one go, because he'll be a dandy. The ears of a mature buck will be 9 or 10 inches long, allowing you to make this comparison with an antler tine or part of the rack. Look for brow tines, also known as eye guards, if you want a high-scoring buck. Many muleys are weak in this category, unlike whitetails, and have absent or very short brow tines. A buck with matching 5-inch brow tines, for example, will have 10 inches added to the score.

Make no mistake – if you're a whitetail deer hunter and have never hunted muleys before, you'll be impressed with the antlers of even a below-average buck, such as one with a very modest 18-inch rack. The height and forks of a mule deer's antlers make him look very large compared to a whitetail. That being the case, you'll be tempted to shoot at the first buck you see, which is precisely why you need to do some homework before your hunt. The more mounts you can look at, the better. I can recall many hunts when first-time mule deer hunters shot the first deer that came along on opening day, and lamented that

107

250 Station Drive
Missoula, MT 59801
(406) 542-1888

BOONE AND CROCKETT CLUB®
OFFICIAL SCORING SYSTEM FOR NORTH AMERICAN BIG GAME TROPHIES

TYPICAL
MULE DEER AND BLACKTAIL DEER

MINIMUM SCORES	AWARDS	ALL-TIME
mule deer	180	190
Columbia blacktail	125	135
Sitka blacktail	100	108

KIND OF DEER (check one)
- [X] mule deer
- [ ] Columbia blacktail
- [ ] Sitka blacktail

Detail of Point
Measurement

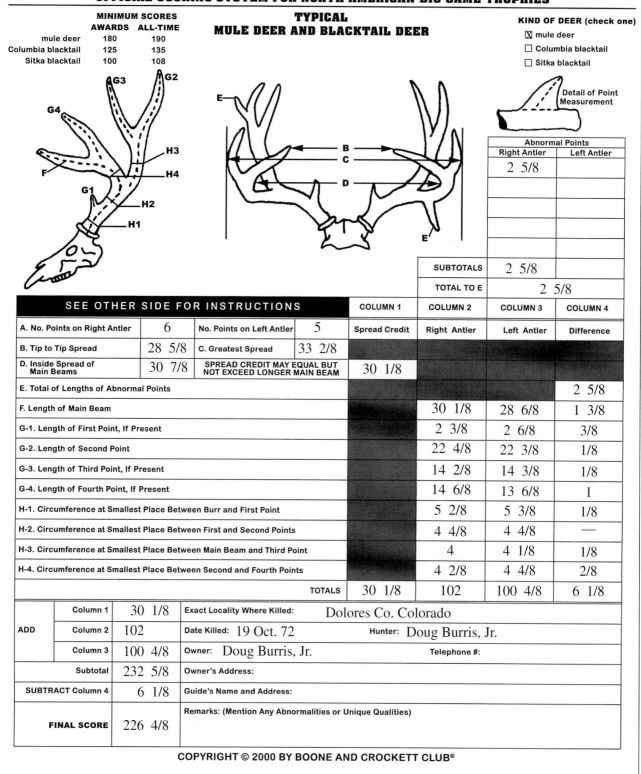

Abnormal Points	
Right Antler	Left Antler
2 5/8	
SUBTOTALS 2 5/8	
TOTAL TO E 2 5/8	

SEE OTHER SIDE FOR INSTRUCTIONS			COLUMN 1	COLUMN 2	COLUMN 3	COLUMN 4
A. No. Points on Right Antler	6	No. Points on Left Antler 5	Spread Credit	Right Antler	Left Antler	Difference
B. Tip to Tip Spread	28 5/8	C. Greatest Spread 33 2/8				
D. Inside Spread of Main Beams	30 7/8	SPREAD CREDIT MAY EQUAL BUT NOT EXCEED LONGER MAIN BEAM	30 1/8			
E. Total of Lengths of Abnormal Points						2 5/8
F. Length of Main Beam				30 1/8	28 6/8	1 3/8
G-1. Length of First Point, If Present				2 3/8	2 6/8	3/8
G-2. Length of Second Point				22 4/8	22 3/8	1/8
G-3. Length of Third Point, If Present				14 2/8	14 3/8	1/8
G-4. Length of Fourth Point, If Present				14 6/8	13 6/8	1
H-1. Circumference at Smallest Place Between Burr and First Point				5 2/8	5 3/8	1/8
H-2. Circumference at Smallest Place Between First and Second Points				4 4/8	4 4/8	—
H-3. Circumference at Smallest Place Between Main Beam and Third Point				4	4 1/8	1/8
H-4. Circumference at Smallest Place Between Second and Fourth Points				4 2/8	4 4/8	2/8
TOTALS			30 1/8	102	100 4/8	6 1/8

ADD			
	Column 1	30 1/8	**Exact Locality Where Killed:** Dolores Co. Colorado
	Column 2	102	**Date Killed:** 19 Oct. 72 **Hunter:** Doug Burris, Jr.
	Column 3	100 4/8	**Owner:** Doug Burris, Jr. **Telephone #:**
	Subtotal	232 5/8	**Owner's Address:**
SUBTRACT Column 4		6 1/8	**Guide's Name and Address:**
FINAL SCORE		226 4/8	**Remarks:** (Mention Any Abnormalities or Unique Qualities)

Reprinted courtesy of the Boone and Crockett Club, 250 Station Drive, Missoula, MT, 59801; (406) 542-1888; www.boone-crockett.org

decision the rest of the hunt when their pals brought in much larger bucks.

It's tough to pass on a fairly good buck, hoping to spot a bigger one later. All too often a hunter lets a buck walk and never sees a bigger one for the duration of the hunt, but that's the risk one takes. Some hunters will pass bucks for the entire hunt, and finally take a "meat" buck on the last day. A true purist will go home with nothing rather than a lesser animal.

In many of my hunting camps, we'd often declare that only a big four-point buck would be a worthy quarry on the first day or two of the season. If no buck of that stature showed up, we'd reduce the standards as the hunt progressed, and on the last day, any one-horned spike had best watch his back trail.

There are very definitely some specific times of the year to hunt trophy bucks with a better chance of seeing one. Some states have very early firearms seasons in September, when bucks are gathered in bachelor groups and are typically hanging out in high elevations. These are most often limited-entry hunts or backcountry hunts where tags must be drawn in a lottery. Finding these bachelor herds this time of year can be tough, since deer are often living in very remote regions. Bowhunters commonly hunt these earlier seasons as a matter of course in most western states. The transition season, or the period between the early season and migration, is the toughest time to find a big muley. Hunters are out in full force, and wary bucks are tucked into their hideouts. The late season is by far the best time to find the mega-buck, because two important natural factors make him more vulnerable than usual. The most significant is the rut, which occurs in most areas from mid-November to mid-December. The migration is the other factor, but-may not take place unless there's adequate snow in the higher elevations to move muleys to winter ranges where they're more accessible to hunters. Complicating the matter is the fact that most states have no general seasons that extend into the rut. There are either no hunts at all, or a limited-entry tag via a lottery draw is required.

Wherever and however you hunt, remember that a big muley with outsized antlers has earned a PhD degree in survival and escape strategy. He's no pushover, and will quickly earn your respect and admiration.

I, _____Arnold O. Haugen_____, certify that I have measured this trophy on __2 / 27 / 1974__
PRINT NAME   MM/DD/YYYYY

at _____Grash Tucker Inc._____   Atlanta   GA
STREET ADDRESS   CITY   STATE/PROVINCE

and that these measurements and data are, to the best of my knowledge and belief, made in accordance with the instructions given.

Witness: _____B. A. Fashingbauer_____   Signature: _____Arnold O. Haugen_____   I.D. Number [ ][ ][ ][ ]
                                                      B&C OFFICIAL MEASURER

INSTRUCTIONS FOR MEASURING TYPICAL MULE AND BLACKTAIL DEER

All measurements must be made with a 1/4-inch wide flexible steel tape to the nearest one-eighth of an inch. (Note: A flexible steel cable can be used to measure points and main beams only.) Enter fractional figures in eighths, without reduction. Official measurements cannot be taken until the antlers have air dried for at least 60 days after the animal was killed.

A. Number of Points on Each Antler: To be counted a point, the projection must be at least one inch long, with length exceeding width at one inch or more of length. All points are measured from tip of point to nearest edge of beam. Beam tip is counted as a point but not measured as a point.

B. Tip to Tip Spread is measured between tips of main beams.

C. Greatest Spread is measured between perpendiculars at a right angle to the center line of the skull at widest part, whether across main beams or points.

D. Inside Spread of Main Beams is measured at a right angle to the center line of the skull at widest point between main beams. Enter this measurement again as the Spread Credit if it is less than or equal to the length of the longer main beam; if greater, enter longer main beam length for Spread Credit.

E. Total of Lengths of all Abnormal Points: Abnormal Points are those non-typical in location such as points originating from a point (exception: G-3 originates from G-2 in perfectly normal fashion) or from bottom or sides of main beam, or any points beyond the normal pattern of five (including beam tip) per antler. Measure each abnormal point in usual manner and enter in appropriate blanks.

F. Length of Main Beam is measured from the center of the lowest outside edge of burr over the outer side to the most distant point of the Main Beam. The point of beginning is that point on the burr where the center line along the outer side of the beam intersects the burr, then following generally the line of the illustration.

G-1-2-3-4. Length of Normal Points: Normal points are the brow tines and the upper and lower forks as shown in the illustration. They are measured from nearest edge of main beam over outer curve to tip. Lay the tape along the outer curve of the beam so that the top edge of the tape coincides with the top edge of the beam on both sides of point to determine the baseline for point measurement. Record point lengths in appropriate blanks.

H-1-2-3-4. Circumferences are taken as detailed in illustration for each measurement. If brow point is missing, take H-1 and H-2 at smallest place between burr and G-2. If G-3 is missing, take H-3 halfway between the base and tip of G-2. If G-4 is missing, take H-4 halfway between G-2 and tip of main beam.

AN OFFICIAL BOONE AND CROCKETT CLUB SCORE SHEET (opposite page) is used to document trophy mule deer. All measurements are taken by an official scorer, following the instructions shown above, and must be witnessed by another party.

Late-Season Hunting

Most general mule deer seasons occur in mid-October throughout the West. This is a time when hunter numbers are at their peaks, and the woods are crowded with people, especially on public land close to good access roads. Many people erroneously believe that this is the time to be hunting since all the good bucks won't survive, and most will be taken by opening-day hunters. Nothing could be farther from the truth. Although indeed some big bucks are taken during the general season, most of these taken are yearlings or small bucks that haven't yet learned to escape.

The late season as defined here occurs after the general season, usually in early to late November. Depending on the latitude, elevation and climate, the late season may or may not involve migration and deep or at least persistent snow. For example, hunts in Arizona, Nevada and parts of California may be warm and dry, even though they're held in late fall.

The major factor to consider during a late hunt is the rut, since muleys begin breeding from early to mid-November throughout much of their range. In mountain country, bucks may leave the upper elevations with or without the presence of snow if does are in the lowlands. Some bucks will linger if does stay high.

Finding deer late in the season may mean a serious physical effort if the weather turns bad or snow is deep. In migration areas, bucks may be at lower elevations, but that doesn't necessarily mean that they'll be an easy walk from your vehicle. You might have a several-mile hike to find them. It's also possible that some of the best hunting will be on private land where you might not have access. A solution is to hunt public land surrounding those private sectors. The farther you walk, the better your chance of finding good bucks, but be sure you have an updated map to keep you aligned on public land.

Since the rut is a factor in late-season hunting, be on the lookout for rubs. These aren't as significant as whitetail rubs, but they point out areas where mule deer have passed. Many times a buck will rub in an area he's comfortable in, often in the central part of his winter home range. Don't confuse elk rubs with deer rubs. The latter will be much fresher, since the last of the elk rubs will have occurred during their breeding season, which is September through early October. Muleys will rub trees and saplings to remove the velvet from their antlers, but those rubs aren't as violent as those in the breeding season. Mule deer also do not make scrapes. If you see a scrape in an area whitetails share with mule deer, you can assume the scrape was made by a whitetail.

If you spot a bunch of does that are feeding and somewhat visible, keep your eye on them from time to time if you can. Get up on a ridge or promontory early in the morning and look for herds of feeding deer. If you spot them, look for a tending buck. In the peak of the rut, practically every group of does will have an obvious buck close by. That buck, however, may not be the dominant male. Quite often a much bigger buck will be out of sight, bedded nearby, until a doe comes into estrus. Then he'll make his move, running off the lesser buck. Trying to move within range of a herd of deer may be a formidable challenge because of the extra eyes, ears and noses. It may be possible to sneak as closely as possible, and then let the deer pass closer to you, if you've been able to figure their route. This is especially true with deer that are feeding in the open during early-morning hours and are headed for bedding areas shortly after daybreak.

In the late season, expect to see a muley buck any time of the day. This is the one time of year that deer don't stick to traditional feeding and bedding schedules. Mature mule deer bucks are great vagabonds, wandering incessantly until they locate their objective – a doe in heat. A rutting buck may walk miles a day. Exceptions are bucks that hang out with very large herds of does. The males have nowhere to go, since plenty of does are close by. This is especially true in ranchland and agricultural areas where deer are concentrated in fields. It's not uncommon to see a hundred or more does in a single field.

Late in the season is the choice timeframe for most serious trophy hunters, but the weather may be a serious hindrance. However, the opportunity at a wallhanger is a small price to pay for the discomfort. Bear in mind that many states don't offer late seasons because big bucks are vulnerable. You might have to draw a tag in a limited-entry unit to get one of the coveted November or December tags – if indeed they're available. Whether you're looking for the buck of your dreams or a deer for the freezer, think late and avoid the crowds during the general season. The reward may be worth it.

Common Mule Deer Hunting Errors

There are all sorts of reasons why a hunt might be unsuccessful, but making avoidable mistakes should never be any of them. Of all the big-game species in the U.S., I think muleys are the most misunderstood, not only by nonresidents who have little or no experi-ence hunting them, but also by locals who should know better.

The biggest mistake is the widespread notion that muleys are dumb. This is typically the opinion offered by hunters who have pursued whitetails all their lives, and then visited mule deer country and observed mule deer in their more open habitat. It's true that because they're more visible, mule deer are more readily spotted in much of their habitat, and it's also true that they aren't as nervous as whitetails, but are more complacent. Having said that, I'm convinced, as are many other hunters who pursue muleys extensively, that big bucks are as wary and elusive as any big whitetail. Mule deer have evolved into a far more cautious species than they were just 30 years ago. I can recall big bucks standing in the sagebrush, looking boldly at hunters and never attempting to run off. Those were the good old days. Now, to be successful, a hunter must be aware of mule deer behavior, be persistent, and give bucks credit for being wary.

There's an interesting belief that muleys always stop and look back at the hunter when they're running off, providing an easy shot. This happens occasionally, but is the exception more than the rule. Bucks indeed had the habit of stopping to look years ago, but that behavior became more infrequent as the deer began adapting new behavior patterns. Don't count on deer looking, but be prepared in case they do. Get set up with your rifle on a solid rest in the event the quarry stops just before going over a ridge. Wildlife experts believe this behavior is due to deer making a final evaluation of danger, thus giving them escape options.

Are you interested in meeting up with a 30-inch buck? Of course you are, and so is everyone else. Unfortunately, there's a common assumption that if you hunt hard enough, you'll find that 30-incher. That's a grievous error, because those bucks might not exist where you hunt for two reasons. First, as fully described elsewhere in this book, a buck's antler configuration is largely determined by his genes. There are many places where even an old buck won't have wide antlers simply because of his genetic makeup. Second, the vast majority of bucks don't live long enough to attain large antlers. A deer can have great genes, and great food, but if he doesn't survive a few hunting seasons, he'll never own a massive

rack. If you're really serious about that 30-incher, do some research and hunt in places that support such bucks.

You've probably heard that rutting muleys are dumber than fenceposts. Everyone knows that, or at least they believe it's true because that's the word on the street. Fact is, mule deer in the rut are as vulnerable as any breeding male, whether it's a whitetail, moose or elk. They lose much of their caution at certain times, but are far from stupid. You might have to contend with horrid weather conditions to find that big rutting buck, and when you do, don't be surprised to learn that he'll disappear like smoke, just as he would any other time of the year.

Always ask permission to hunt on private land.

The biggest error committed by mule deer hunters is looking for deer within 300 yards of a pickup truck. Many hunters are too lazy or too uninformed to hike and expend some physical effort. This is especially true in country that offers visibility. Hunters believe that any deer around will be easily spotted. I've known hunters who are road hunting champions. These guys have vehicles specially rigged for hunting, and carry enough coffee, food and gasoline to last all day. They leave the warm interior of the truck only to walk 50 yards to look over a ledge or nearby ridgetop, and a 2-minute hike is their max. Predictably, these people seldom see mature bucks, and more often than not, will end up shooting spikes or forkhorns. Road hunting is a major way of hunting mule deer in every state. Perhaps we should be thankful for that, since the bigger bucks easily go undetected. That means more deer for those who are willing to work for them. Hooray for road hunters!

After the Shot

If all goes well and your bullet, arrow or saboted bullet finds its mark, your mule deer hunt will be successful from the standpoint of the consumptive angle. Since there's no such thing as catch-and-release in hunting, the reward is tangible. The objective at that point is to get your meat from the woods to the freezer, and in such a way that it will be not only edible, but good to eat.

The first order of business when you approach your deer is NOT to tag it, which some folks believe to be the case. Your primary requirement is to make sure it's dead! Approach the animal very cautiously from the uphill side where you can view it from a distance. Look at its eyes first – if they're closed, rest assured the animal is still alive. If the eyes are open, chances

114

Once the mule deer is expired, you must tag it IMMEDIATELY; but don't procrastinate in order to take pictures or round up some buddies. A game warden who shows up won't find any humor in an untagged deer, no matter what the circumstances.

Once tagged, you should quickly begin the job of field dressing, regardless of the situation you're confronted with. Now you must become a meat processor, but you won't have a nice, clean environment in which to work. Moreover, you'll probably be operating in thick brush, perhaps on a steep slope, or perhaps in a driving rainstorm or blizzard. Those are aspects you can't control. What you CAN control is the knowledge you'll need to get the chore accomplished, and having the appropriate tools to do so.

FIELD-DRESSING TIPS

Venison is one of the finest meats gathered by hunters, but it can taste simply awful when you sit down at the dinner table to enjoy your reward. Improper dressing and field care are among the chief culprits. Two key words that you must abide by are cool and clean. Cool is absolutely mandatory; clean is always a good idea to avoid localized meat waste.

Once your prize has expired, bacteria immediately begin to decompose it. Speed is of the utmost importance. You should have the entrails out of the carcass within an hour after it hits the ground. Any longer and it will begin to bloat, even during cold weather. The following technique has worked for me for 40 years, including everything from antelope to mule deer to moose.

If possible, drag the carcass into the shade to keep sunlight from it. Position it so the hindquarters are lower than the head. Cut around the anus, preferably with a long-bladed knife that will penetrate. The idea is to completely free the intestine from the connective tissue in the anal wall. Begin opening the stomach by making an initial slit at the anus and very carefully working your knife toward the throat, this time cutting only the skin layer. If you want to have the head mounted, stop the cut well below the brisket. As you cut, make the incision to the side of the testicles and penis or udders (in the case of a doe) since evidence of sex may be legally required.

Next, retrace this cut; this slit will open the cavity. Start this cut where you circled the anus, working toward the throat. Guide your knife blade between your second and third fingers, holding your fingers facing up, but pressing the stomach down, allowing you to cut only the membrane. Take care not to puncture the stomach or intestines. As you cut, the internal pressure will push the stomach out. That's natural. When you've reached the breastbone, you'll

are good the deer has expired, but that's not always true. And if the eyes are blinking, it won't take a rocket scientist to realize the animal is still alive.

If you believe the animal is alive, back off and find an angle where you can administer a safe shot to dispatch it. Aim for the spinal cord under the chin if you can. This will insure a humane ending, with no loss of meat. A shot to the body may not perform the task, and you'll end up damaging plenty of meat.

have an option of cutting through it up to the throat, or eliminating this cut. If you use a saw, keep the saw blade angled so the tip doesn't keep digging into the cavity as you work. If the deer is small, a stout pocket knife will work instead of a saw. Be sure you cut away from you for safety. Never straddle the deer and work the knife toward you.

With the incision complete from the anus to the neck, reach in and cut away the diaphragm wall that is connected to the spine. Continue to cut away any connective tissues that hold the entrails to the rib cage, being careful not to pierce them. Reach as high as you can and sever the windpipe. Pull on it firmly with both hands, and it should tear free, pulling the organs, stomach, and intestines with it. Allow the innards to roll out and downhill, cutting any connective muscles and tissues as required. Take special care when freeing the urine-filled bladder located just forward of the pelvis where the hindquarters join. Gently pull it away, allowing it to fall out intact. Trim away the kidneys, excessive fat, and bloodshot tissue at this point.

If you must leave the deer and return for it later, be sure it's in a shady spot. Lay it on its back, spreading the cavity with sticks. The idea now is to allow it to cool as rapidly as possible. If possible, hang it from a tree, provided it's in the shade. The breeze will cool it more quickly. At this point you can wipe away dirt and continue to do some trimming. Be wary of wildlife such as ravens, coyotes, magpies, jays, bears and other creatures. If you lay the deer on the ground, cover it lightly with branches to discourage critters, but allow air to circulate.

Skinning a deer immediately isn't required if the air temperature is cool. It's better to put off skinning until you're ready to process the animal, since the carcass dries, and much of the outer layer will be lost. During bitterly cold weather in the North, the carcass may freeze solidly if the animal is left overnight, requiring thawing before being skinned. During hot weather, the carcass should be skinned immediately, preferably as soon as it's field-dressed.

Leaving the Carcass Unattended

If it gets too dark to transport the dressed carcass, or if you intend to go for help, be aware that you're taking a chance by leaving the deer. Animals and birds will be a nuisance, requiring you to take steps to prevent loss or damage. In mule deer country, ravens or magpies will be a pesky problem, and in some areas, buzzards could be a serious threat. To keep birds away, drag the carcass into the shadiest spot you can find and lay it on thick branches to allow air to circulate underneath. Then cover the carcass with plenty of brush, especially thick boughs of evergreens that you've cut from the bottoms of trees. Never cut saplings if you can help it. Pile the boughs so that air can circulate freely, and cover the carcass entirely so no meat is exposed. Birds will be very enterprising, and can often get to meat that you thought was amazingly well-protected.

Once I killed a nice five-by-five muley in Montana and covered the carcass with boughs. I covered the heart and liver nearby with at least 10 inches of packed snow, and when I returned with help 6 hours later, ravens had located the meat and were merrily working away. They'd eaten all the heart and more than half the liver.

In the case of four-footed predators, you'll need to worry about black bears and coyotes. Mountain lions prefer to kill their own deer and normally aren't a problem. In some parts of mule deer country, wolves are well established, and grizzlies are abundant. In the case of the former, you shouldn't have to worry about wolves making off with your deer, though it's possible. A grizzly will indeed feast on your deer, and you won't have any recourse if it does. If you're in grizzly country and you must leave the deer overnight, drag the carcass into a large opening where you can view it from a distance when you return. That way, you'll be able to see if it's disturbed. To protect a deer from coyotes and bears, you'll need to hang it high in a tree and far enough away from the trunk so a bear can't reach it.

As much as I hate to say it, there are a few sorry humans who dress in hunter's clothing and are thieves. From time to time we hear about people who steal unattended deer. To help foil these individuals, take plenty of photos of your deer (if it's a buck) from several angles, so it can be identified if you catch up to the culprits. Also, cut a deep slit somewhere in the carcass and insert a coin whose date you've memorized. If you see your deer in someone else's possession, call a law enforcement officer and retrieve the coin with the officer watching.

Getting It Out

The easiest way to get a deer out is to drive up to it and load it in your pickup or ATV. In the case of the latter, be certain you're obeying the travel rules if you're on public land. On private land, ranchers may also have specific guidelines as to where you may or may not drive ATV's. Whether you hunt public or private land, be absolutely sure you know what the restrictions are.

Another easy way is to load your deer on a horse, and carry it out to a road. Let's say your deer falls where you must somehow transport it through the woods by yourself or with one companion. Dragging it is the most common way to move it, but that can be an ordeal if much (or any) of the route is uphill. There are a few things you can do to assist this procedure. First, always drag the animal headfirst, or the hide and legs will snag constantly in the brush. Pull the front legs as far forward as you can and secure them tightly to the head with rope or strong twine.

It's tempting to grab an antler and pull, but that's the tough way because you're using your hands and arms, which will tire quickly. Instead, use a drag harness that fits over your upper torso. You'll be able to pull with your shoulders and back, and have a far easier time. Two people pulling at the same time will help enormously. Drag harnesses are simple straps that are sold in most outdoor catalogs or sporting goods stores. If you don't have one, merely make a loop on a rope and put it over your shoulders so it rests under your arms. Tie the other end of the rope to the deer's head or antlers so the animal is just a few feet behind you and isn't so close that it interferes with your walking. Bend forward and pull. Wear a couple shirts or a jacket to keep the rope from causing discomfort.

If you're alone or with a pal who physically can't help much and you have an uphill drag, try this simple trick: cut the deer in two pieces so there's a front half and rear half. Drag each half separately. Years ago, my pal and I were faced with a very steep uphill drag with a very large Wyoming buck. We each grabbed an antler and pulled mightily, making only a few feet of progress each time we heaved. Our destination was still a half-mile away when I had the bright idea of reducing the load. I cut the carcass in two pieces, and though we had to make two trips, we didn't need to worry about a hernia or worse.

Nowadays a number of companies are making specialized drag devices which are simply synthetic sleds that you load the deer on. These can be rectangular heavy duty tarps with grommets to lash the carcass to, with a pull rope affixed to a harness. Some are plastic type sleds that slide easily over rough terrain.

A wheeled cart is a simple solution. These work very well, and I've been using them for years. The disadvantage is the need to go to the vehicle, retrieve the cart, and return to the carcass with it since it's too unwieldy to bring along while you're hunting. But this added chore is worth it when your buck is in the bottom of a canyon and your truck is parked a mile or more away. Commercial carts are normally sturdily built and will last a long time.

A pole carry will work well if there are two of you and neither of you has a shoulder or back ailment.

Find a sturdy pole, but not one that's too heavy, since the added weight is an unnecessary burden. Lash the deer to the pole tightly so it doesn't swing side to side, throwing you off balance. Put a jacket or some type of padding on your shoulder under the pole to ease the strain.

Boning the deer where it fell is the best way to reduce unnecessary weight. By doing so, you'll leave behind the hide, bones, head, feet, fat and bloodshot meat, taking only the edible flesh. You can reduce a buck that weighs 200 pounds on the hoof to around 60 to 80 pounds of meat. To accommodate the meat, use a sturdy game bag. As you work, place chunks of meat on a clean surface such as a rock or log, or a space blanket, small tarp, or other material from your backpack. Lay it in the shade so it will cool. The idea is to eliminate heat quickly; this should take less than an hour. Then place the meat in the bag, and hang the bag in a tree as you work to continue the chilling process.

SKINNING AND CAPING TIPS

This is a simple process, and is best done with the animal hanging from its rear legs. Ideally, use a metal or heavy-duty plastic gambrel that will hold the animal by the hocks. Cut a slit in each hock and put the hooked ends of the gambrel in each slit. If you don't have a gambrel, use a stout branch. With a rope tied to the middle of the gambrel, toss the rope over a tree limb and carefully raise the animal off the ground until it's hanging so you can easily reach the uppermost part of the carcass. A small portable block and tackle will greatly help raise the carcass.

Make a shallow slit from inside the hindquarter up to the tail area. Begin peeling and cutting the hide away, and cut off the tail. Continue working down toward the head. You should be able to peel most of the hide without using a knife. Work your fingers under the skin and pull hard, cutting the spots that won't peel easily. When you reach the brisket, make a slit from each knee up to the center cut, and continue peeling down to the neck. Keep going, and when the hide is removed as far as the throat, cut the head off under the chin, retaining as much of the neck on the carcass as possible. Protect the skinned carcass by wrapping it completely with several layers of cheesecloth. Better yet, put it in a deer bag made exclusively to hold an entire carcass. Most of these bags are reusable. They can be laundered after each use and will last for years.

Some hunters will skin a deer and cut the hide off at the neck, leaving the head attached. Then they'll wrap the body in cheesecloth, tying the material off at the neck to protect it from flies, or they'll likewise with a meat bag. There's a problem here: flies will enter the carcass via the mouth or nostrils, working their way into the rib area. They'll lay their eggs, unbeknown to you, and you'll make the nasty discovery of finding maggots chomping on your carcass days afterward. To avoid this, put the entire carcass in the meat bag and tie it tightly. I don't use cheesecloth anymore because flies will often lay their eggs through the flimsy material.

If your buck is bound for your wall, you can either cape it yourself if you know how (but don't try it unless you're competent at this task), or you can take the head to a taxidermist. To do the latter, stop your belly cut well below the brisket as you field-dress. Make a slit up the center of the back well up into the neck, and make slits from inside the knees up and around the entire carcass, leaving plenty of hide. Peel the hide until it's all free, including the neck, and cut off the head as close to the chin as possible. Waste no time getting the head and attached hide to a taxidermist. If you cape it completely, pour plenty of salt on the cape and place it in the shade.

Be aware that every state has different regulations regarding evidence of sex. In most, you'll need to leave at least one testicle or udder (in case of a doe), naturally attached to the carcass. It cannot be removed until the carcass has been delivered to a bona fide processor or it arrives at your home if you're going to process it yourself. In the case of boned meat, the law usually requires you to leave the evidence attached to a major part of the meat. Again, carefully check the regulations before you remove the testicles or udders. Of course, if the carcass is intact with the head intact, that in itself is evidence of sex.

GETTING YOUR MEAT HOME

Many hunters take their deer to a local processor and either take it home with them after it's done, or have it shipped afterward. Save yourself some problems by checking with processors before you hunt. In many small towns, carcasses can't be cut up for several days, and in many cases there won't be any room for more deer. Always have two or three processors located. Then there's the problem of getting your deer on the last day, and not having enough time for the processor to cut it up so you can take it home. In that case, you'll have to ship it, which can be expensive, or take it home intact.

Be sure to tell the processor specifically how you want your meat cut, i.e, how many pounds of burger per package, how many steaks, how big you want the roasts to be, etc. In most cases, you can trade your meat for sausage, jerky, salami, and other types of meats. You'll be charged additionally, and the fee depends on the type of meat you want. You can trade only the equal weight of the boned meat your animal yields, plus an additional 10 percent or so that usually includes the suet and spices that are added. You cannot buy wild game according to most state laws, but you can trade it. In other words, if your buck yields 60 pounds of meat and you want it all made into sausage, all you can legally get back in the trade is about 65 pounds. Check with the processor in advance as to the details.

I always travel with a couple of coolers to get my meat back, whether I'm flying or driving. I'll often put chilled meat in a cooler if I intend on flying and I have less than 8 hours to get home from the hunt area. Many times I'll bone a deer into big chunks, chill it, and cut it up as I want when I get home, or, if I don't have time to cut it up, take it to my processor. If it's frozen in big chunks, then I'll have to thaw it and then cut it up, refreezing it again. I avoid that if I can. If I'm driving, and I have a long trip, I'll leave chilled meat in a cooler for several days if the air temperature is cool. I drive a pickup, and the cooler stays in the bed (which is covered by a topper) with the lid propped up. If you have a Suburban, the inside of your vehicle will be warm. Keep the cooler lid closed, and when you stop at a motel, open the lid to let the night air cool it down. Of course, if you're traveling in warm weather, you have no options for chilling the meat. It's best to freeze it and lay dry ice on top, closing the cooler lid tightly.

If you travel by plane, be sure you inform the clerk that you have dry ice in a cooler. This is a restricted item, and it's best to find out in advance what the airline regulations are. The maximum weight allowed by most airlines per cooler is 70 pounds. You can easily exceed that weight if you have a large cooler. If you do, you'll be charged extra, or the cooler will be air freighted, and probably not shipped on the same flight you're on. Avoid those problems by weighing the cooler before you tape it shut.

If you intend to bring your deer home whole, be sensitive to nonhunters who might find a dead animal in full view distasteful. Some hunters have a bit of an arrogant attitude, believing that it's their right to do whatever they want with their animal. In today's society that's a mistake. I believe it's far better to transport your animal so it's out of sight – not from the standpoint of hiding it because we've done something wrong, but to respect the feelings of others. And remember, we're in the minority – big time. Let's not shoot ourselves in the foot.

Venison Tips

If you've ever wondered why a deer steak doesn't taste like a beef steak, it's because it's not supposed to. Venison tastes like venison, beef tastes like beef, pork tastes like pork. Venison has a unique flavor all its own. But if you've heard that venison has an off-taste because it wasn't properly cared for in the field, that might be only partially true. Many times I've walked up to a muley buck in the rut and noted a most disagreeable odor, simply because the buck was breeding and his body chemistry had changed. It's also true that the flesh of a rutting buck might taste extremely gamey, regardless of field care.

There are a number of reasons why a deer might taste gamier than usual. The rut, as just discussed, is a major factor. I've taken big muley bucks in September and found them delectable. I can't say I've ever taken a mild-tasting mature buck during the rut in late November. The age of a deer is also a primary reason. It's not easy to shoot an old buck, because very few live beyond 3 or 4 years, but many does are extremely old. Since they don't wear antlers, it's impossible to tell how old they are when you squeeze the trigger. The diet of an animal might also determine its eating qualities. An animal subsisting on bitter plants might indeed be gamey tasting. And then we have the field-care issue. It's abundantly clear that improper field handling can have a major impact on a deer's flavor. The need to dress the animal immediately after it expires and to cool the carcass quickly are the two key issues. Each may be extremely difficult to control if the circumstances aren't right. For example, a deer might run off and die, leaving a minimum blood trail or none at all. If the hunter doesn't recover it for several hours, it may be bloated, or beginning to bloat, and the quality of the flesh will be adversely affected. It's also common to kill a deer and be unable to cool the carcass properly, such as during hot weather in a camp where you can't get the carcass into a cool environment for a few days.

So what do you do if you have a deer that's marginally fit for human consumption, or at least an animal that's on the gamey side? One solution is to trade it in to a processor for an equal amount of venison sausage. That's the easy way out, and it always works, though it will cost money. Another option is to process it yourself, using techniques that will render it less gamey. One tip is to grind the meat yourself into burger, adding spices that will neutralize the gamey flavor. Another is to use a variety of marinades, and another is to use the meat in chili and stew where other ingredients will disguise the taste.

It's also necessary to eliminate all the fat on the flesh, since the fat imparts a nasty taste. Likewise with hair from the pelt. Even one wisp of hair will add a bitter taste to the meat. If you have the animal processed, don't allow the meat to be sectioned with a saw. The bone dust from the saw will give the meat an off-taste. Roasts are the most difficult of all the meats to tame, because a roast is a large chunk and it's tough to penetrate it with marinades and spices. If you think your deer will be strong, tell your processor not to cut roasts. He will want to cut as many as possible, since that reduces processing time, and profit is dependent on how many deer he can cut up in a day.

Many recipes will help turn your gamey cuts into unexpected delights. Here are my favorites, which will transform any awful cut into a culinary feast.

Venison with Fresh Ginger

2 pounds deer steak
5-6 slices fresh ginger root, peeled and cut in 1-inch
    slices
⅛ cup fresh ginger root, peeled and minced
2 medium onions, sliced
2 cloves garlic, minced
1 teaspoon sugar
1 cup soy sauce
2 to 3 tablespoons vegetable oil
2 tablespoons cornstarch

Cut deer steaks, across the grain, into 2-inch strips. Layer venison, sliced onions, garlic, and ⅛ cup ginger root in glass bowl. Combine soy sauce and sugar and pour liquid over meat. Cover and refrigerate 45 minutes to 1 hour.

Heat oil and cook 5 to 6 slices fresh ginger root until browned and flavor is released into oil. Remove and discard these ginger slices. Drain the majority of soy sauce from the meat and onion marinade. Add meat, onions, garlic and ginger slices to oil in skillet. Saute 2 to 3 minutes, then sprinkle cornstarch over meat and stir. Continue cooking until meat is completely cooked. Add additional soy sauce to taste. Serves 6.

Western Chili

2 pounds ground venison
1 cup cooking oil
1 cup chopped onion
2 cloves garlic, minced
1 large green pepper, chopped
3 tablespoons chili powder
2 cups whole tomatoes
1 cup tomato sauce
1 cup water
1 teaspoon salt
1 tablespoon flour mixed with 2 tablespoons water
3 cups cooked kidney beans

Brown venison in oil in a Dutch oven until meat loses its pink color. Add onion, garlic, and green pepper. Cook for 5 minutes. Add chili powder, tomatoes, tomato sauce, water and salt. Simmer for 2 hours. Add the flour paste and cook until mixture thickens. Add the kidney beans and cook another 15 minutes. Serves 6 to 8.

Note: Both these recipes adapted from Jim Zumbo's *Amazing Venison Recipes Cookbook*. For information, call 1-800-673-4868.

Bacon-wrapped Tenderloin

Recipes

The following recipes, along with hundreds of additional venison recipes can be found in the book, *Venison Cookery*, another title in the *The Complete Hunter* series. Phone 1-800-328-3895 for more information.

BACON-WRAPPED TENDERLOIN

¼ *teaspoon salt*
¼ *teaspoon onion powder*
¼ *teaspoon garlic powder*
¼ *teaspoon pepper*
  Venison tenderloin (about 1 lb.)
2 strips bacon
1 tablespoon butter or margarine

3 to 4 servings

In small bowl, combine salt, onion powder, garlic powder and pepper. Rub all sides of tenderloin evenly with spice mixture. Wrap bacon strips in a spiral around tenderloin, securing ends with wooden picks.

Heat 10-inch cast-iron skillet over medium heat. Melt butter in skillet. Add tenderloin. Cook for 4 to 6 minutes, or until meat is browned on all sides. Reduce heat to low or set skillet off direct heat. Cover. Cook for 12 to 15 minutes, or until meat is desired doneness, turning tenderloin occasionally. Let stand for 5 minutes before slicing.

Per Serving: Calories: 226 • Protein: 27 g. • Carbohydrate: <1 g. • Fat: 12 g.
• Cholesterol: 112 mg. • Sodium: 300 mg.
Exchanges: 3¼ very lean meat, 2½ fat

CORN-STUFFED ROLLED TOP ROUND ROAST

Stuffing:

2 tablespoons butter or
   margarine
1 small onion, finely chopped
   (¾ cup)
½ cup finely chopped red pepper
1 cup frozen corn kernels,
   defrosted
1 can (4 oz.) minced green chilies
1½ cups crumbled corn bread
½ cup shredded Cheddar cheese
¼ cup snipped fresh cilantro
   leaves
½ teaspoon cumin seed
½ teaspoon salt
¼ to ½ teaspoon crushed red
   pepper flakes

2-to 3-lb. boneless venison top
   round roast, butterflied to
   1-inch thickness
1 tablespoon vegetable oil

8 to 12 servings

Heat oven to 450°F. In 12-inch skillet, melt butter over medium heat. Add onion and pepper. Cook for 3 to 5 minutes, or until vegetables are tender, stirring occasionally. Stir in corn and chilies. Cook for 1 to 2 minutes, or until corn is heated through, stirring frequently. Remove from heat.

Stir in remaining stuffing ingredients. Spread and pack stuffing evenly on roast. Roll up roast jelly-roll-style, rolling with grain of meat. Tie roast at 1-inch intervals, using kitchen string. Place roast on rack in roasting pan. Brush with oil.

Roast for 10 minutes. Reduce heat to 350°F. Roast to desired doneness, 20 to 25 minutes per lb.

Per Serving: Calories: 217 • Protein: 24 g.
• Carbohydrate: 11 g. • Fat: 8 g.
• Cholesterol: 97 mg. • Sodium: 334 mg.
Exchanges: ½ starch, 3 very lean meat, ¼ vegetable, 1¾ fat

WILD RICE SOUP

1 lb. lean ground venison,
   crumbled
½ cup butter or margarine
¼ cup finely chopped onion
¾ cup all-purpose flour
6 cups ready-to-serve chicken
   broth
4 cups cooked wild rice

1 cup shredded carrots
⅓ cup slivered almonds
1 to 2 teaspoons seasoned salt
1 teaspoon freshly ground
   pepper
1½ cups 2% milk
¼ cup dry sherry (optional)

8 servings

In 6-quart Dutch oven or stockpot, cook venison over medium heat for 6 to 8 minutes, or until meat is no longer pink, stirring occasionally. Drain. Remove meat from pot. Set aside. Wipe out pot.

In same pot, melt butter over medium heat. Add onion. Cook for 2 to 3 minutes, or until tender, stirring occasionally. Stir in flour. Cook for 1 minute, stirring constantly. Gradually whisk in broth. Cook for 6 to 8 minutes, or until soup comes to a boil, stirring constantly. Cook for 1 minute, stirring constantly.

Stir in venison, rice, carrots, almonds, salt and pepper. Simmer for 5 minutes, stirring occasionally. Stir in milk and sherry. Cook for 4 to 6 minutes, or until heated through, stirring occasionally. (Do not boil.) Garnish soup with snipped fresh parsley or chives, if desired.

Per Serving: Calories: 431 • Protein: 20 g. • Carbohydrate: 32 g. • Fat: 25 g.
• Cholesterol: 82 mg. • Sodium: 1159 mg.
Exchanges: 1¼ starch, 1½ medium-fat meat, ¼ vegetable, ¼ low-fat milk, 3¼ fat

SNAPPY SLOPPY JOES

2 lbs. lean ground venison,
   crumbled
8 oz. fresh mushrooms, sliced
   (3 cups)
1 medium onion, chopped
   (1 cup)
1 jar (12 oz.) chili sauce
1 cup catsup
½ cup water

1 to 2 tablespoons
   Worcestershire sauce
1 tablespoon fresh horseradish
1 teaspoon red pepper sauce
½ teaspoon garlic powder
½ teaspoon celery seed
½ teaspoon salt
8 to 10 hamburger buns, split

8 to 10 servings

In 6-quart Dutch oven or stockpot, combine venison, mushrooms and onion. Cook over medium heat for 12 to 15 minutes, or until meat is no longer pink, stirring occasionally. Drain.

Stir in remaining ingredients, except buns. Bring to a simmer. Simmer for 20 to 25 minutes, or until flavors are blended and mixture is desired thickness, stirring occasionally. Serve mixture on buns. Serve with dill pickle and tomato slices, if desired.

Per Serving: Calories: 436 • Protein: 23 g. • Carbohydrate: 40 g. • Fat: 21 g.
• Cholesterol: 81 mg. • Sodium: 1169 mg.
Exchanges: 2 starch, 2 medium-fat meat, 2 vegetable, 2 fat

The Future of Mule Deer Hunting

Any discussion on the future of mule deer hunting must first address the issue of the deer itself. Much of that information is covered in another chapter on deer populations, but generally speaking, muleys have been in the spotlight lately inasmuch as some people believe the species is in trouble.

Most big-game species in North America have rebounded nicely from the all-time low populations around the end of the 1800s. Mule deer made a steady recovery from those depressed years but unfortunately there are fewer of them now than there were during the banner years of the 1950s, 60s, and 70s. Their populations undoubtedly will never climb to match those peak years.

As described elsewhere in this book, there are some good reasons for those declines, notably habitat loss, susceptibility to severe winters, diseases, predators and parasites. In some instances, overhunting may have caused temporary decreases, where wildlife officers made management decisions that resulted in too many deer being harvested.

The ever-shrinking habitat is the prime culprit in depressed mule deer numbers. One only has to look at suburbs continually growing outward from western cities and towns, gobbling up land at an incredible rate. Much of that land was once prime winter range, which is critical to mule deer survival, especially during severe winters.

Unlike whitetails, which are thriving in backyards and highly populated suburban areas, muleys are more oriented to wintering in open spaces with less human activity. Muleys can indeed live in and around people in many areas, but prefer to remain in more isolated places. Food sources in the West are also different for muleys, inasmuch as they have more specialized requirements than whitetails. Once the food is removed from the equation because of habitat degradation, mule deer cannot survive.

Controversies exist about the muley's ability to maintain a "pure" species because of its ability to interbreed with whitetails. This hybridization always involves a whitetail buck and a mule deer doe, and the offspring is typically inferior to the point where its chances of survival are poor. As a result, the mule deer doe loses its fawn, while the whitetails continue to produce healthy offspring. Over several generations, it's believed that muleys will slowly lose ground. An extreme theory suggests that muleys will ultimately

lose out completely, but most wildlife scientists don't agree.

If we believe that mule deer will sustain their populations at huntable levels, then it's obvious that the future of mule deer hunting is linked to the overall acceptability of hunting in general. Since muleys are hunted primarily in the western states, where hunting is a way of life, it's doubtful that deer hunting would be impacted by anti-hunting activities. There are exceptions, such as heavily populated California, and along the Interstate 5 corridor in Oregon and Washington, where blacktails thrive.

From a national perspective, the average age of the American hunter is growing older, which doesn't

bode well for hunting anywhere. On the plus side, more women than ever are hunting, giving the hunting image a fresh new look.

Some organizations are working hard to preserve mule deer habitat and to insure the perpetuity of the species in other ways. The Rocky Mountain Elk Foundation (1-800-CALLELK) has spent millions to protect elk habitat throughout the West. By doing so, muleys are also benefactors, since any land protected from development is land that will benefit all species. Another group, the Mule Deer Foundation (1-888-375-DEER) has been struggling for years to become a credible organization, and it appears that now the group is finally well organized and moving

in the right direction. Never before have muleys needed such a helping hand from mankind.

Despite dire predictions from some observers that muleys are in desperate trouble, I don't believe it. Cyclic populations are natural, flowing from peaks to lows, always yielding to natural factors that temporarily reduce mule deer numbers.

I believe mule deer are here to stay, as is the hunt for them. Millions of acres of public land will insure that there will always be untouched habitat, regardless of what's happening in the private sector. That private sector, however, is extremely important to the welfare of muleys, and must be protected at every turn. Mule deer deserve no less.

Index

Creative Publishing international, Inc.
offers a variety of how-to books.

For information call or write:
  Creative Publishing international, Inc.
  Subscriber Books
  5900 Green Oak Drive
  Minnetonka, MN 55343
  1-800-328-3895

Or visit us at:
  www.howtobookstore.com

Contributing Photographers (Note: T=*Top*, C=*Center*, B=*Bottom*, L=*Left*, R=*Right*, i=*inset*)

Erwin & Peggy Bauer
Sequim, WA
© *Erwin & Peggy Bauer: pp. 12B,
13TL, 20L, 80-81, 98-99*

Kathy S. Butt
Portland, TN
© *Kathy S. Butt: pp. 38-39*

Tim Christie
TimChristie.com
© *Tim Christie: pp. 13B, 14, 32-
33, 54, 65, 70, 86, 93*

Michael H. Francis
Billings, MT
© *Michael H. Francis: front cover,
pp. 25, 76, 111*

D. Robert Franz
Morrison, CO
© *D. Robert Franz: pp. 21, 96*

Donald M. Jones
Troy, MT
© *Donald M. Jones: pp. 6, 12TL,
36-37, 42-43, 62-63*

Mark Kayser
Pierre, SD
© *Mark Kayser: back cover-BR,
pp. 16, 18-19, 46, 49, 50-51, 74-
75, 82, 88, 114-115, 122-123*

Lee Kline
Loveland, CO
© *Lee Kline: pp. 26, 78, 90, 100*

Gary Kramer
Willows, CA
© *Gary Kramer: pp. 10-11, 12TR,
13TR*

Bill McRae
Choteau, MT
© *Bill McRae: back cover-CR, pp.
56-57, 66-67, 94, 102-103, 106*

Wyman Meinzer
Benjamin, TX
© *Wyman Meinzer: p. 84*

George Robbins
Powell, WY
© *George Robbins: pp. 28-29*

Wendy Shattil & Bob Rozinski
Denver, CO
© *Wendy Shattil/Bob Rozinski:
back cover-TR, pp. 8-9,
22-23, 24*

Dusan Smetana
DusanSmetana.com
© *Dusan Smetana: p. 72*

Ron Spomer
Bloomington, IN
© *Ron Spomer: back cover-TL,
pp. 17, 20R, 30-31, 52, 58-59,
69, 104-105, 112-113, 113R*

Creative Publishing international is the most complete source of How-To Information for the Outdoorsman

THE COMPLETE HUNTER™ *Series*

- *Advanced Whitetail Hunting*
- *America's Favorite Wild Game Recipes*
- *Bowhunting Equipment & Skills*
- *The Complete Guide to Hunting*
- *Cooking Wild in Kate's Kitchen*
- *Dressing & Cooking Wild Game*
- *Duck Hunting*
- *Elk Hunting*
- *Game Bird Cookery*
- *Mule Deer Hunting*
- *Muzzleloading*
- *Pronghorn Hunting*
- *Upland Game Birds*
- *Venison Cookery*
- *Whitetail Deer*
- *Wild Turkey*

The Freshwater Angler™ Series

- *Advanced Bass Fishing*
- *All-Time Favorite Fish Recipes*
- *The Art of Fly Tying*
- *The Art of Freshwater Fishing*
- *Fishing for Catfish*
- *Fishing Rivers & Streams*
- *Fishing Tips & Tricks*
- *Fishing With Artificial Lures*
- *Fishing With Live Bait*
- *Fly Fishing for Trout in Streams*
- *Largemouth Bass*
- *Modern Methods of Ice Fishing*
- *The New Cleaning & Cooking Fish*
- *Northern Pike & Muskie*
- *Panfish*
- *Smallmouth Bass*
- *Successful Walleye Fishing*
- *Trout*

The Complete FLY FISHERMAN™ Series

- *Fishing Dry Flies – Surface Presentations for Trout in Streams*
- *Fishing Nymphs, Wet Flies & Streamers – Subsurface Techniques for Trout in Streams*
- *Fly-Fishing Equipment & Skills*
- *Fly-Tying Techniques & Patterns*